healing the
hidden self

healing the

hidden self

Barbara Shlemon Ryan

ave maria press **AmP** Notre Dame, Indiana

www.avemariapress.com

International Standard Book Number: 1-59471-033-3

Cover and text design by Katherine Robinson Coleman

Printed and bound in the United States of America.

Library of Congress Cataloging-in-Publication Data

Ryan, Barbara Shlemon.
  Healing the hidden self / Barbara Shlemon Ryan.— Rev. ed.
    p. cm.
  Includes bibliographical references.
  ISBN 1-59471-033-3 (pbk.)
  1. Conduct of life. 2. Spiritual healing. 3. Prayers. I. Title.

BJ1581.2.R93 2005
248.8'6—dc22

2005003356

CONTENTS

FOREWORD

WHEN THIS BOOK WAS ORIGINALLY PUBLISHED in 1982, I hoped it would be of some value to those who were seeking greater emotional and spiritual balance in life. Having been in print continuously since first published, it has greatly exceeded my modest hopes! Many therapists have told me they use it as an adjunct to their counseling sessions. One particular therapist said, "I ask my clients to read a chapter prior to our next appointment and this invariably causes some important life experiences to surface." A university professor gives it as assigned reading for his class in developmental psychology. One woman told me that preceding their annual family vacation, she sent a copy of *Healing the Hidden Self* to each of her parents and siblings. During the week, they spent many hours talking and praying for one another. "We were drawn together as never before and our love for one another has definitely increased."

Whenever I speak at a conference or lead a retreat, I can count on someone coming up to me with a story of how this book healed old memories and fostered renewed hope. Many of the stories involved long-standing emotional hurts that no longer caused the person to feel ashamed. As one man described it, "I thought my life was useless due to the rejection of my father but the prayers in your book have freed me to accept myself and let go of the past."

This revised edition incorporates some of the material I've gleaned since it was first published. I have no doubt that it will inspire many others to accept the healing that is rightfully theirs through the gentle touch of Jesus Christ.

INTRODUCTION

For several years in the 1970s I was employed as a nurse in a Veteran's Administration psychiatric hospital. Each day we would spend time with men and women who were exhibiting various anti-social behavioral problems. The psychiatrist in charge of our unit believed his patients would be aided in overcoming their mental illnesses once they understood the root causes of the problems. Group therapy sessions were designed to elicit information on traumatic experiences. Once we identified these areas, a treatment program was initiated to liberate the patient from the trauma's unhealthy effects.

Unfortunately this method didn't obtain the desired results. Knowing what precipitated the mental problems often produced an added burden of guilt. One patient told me, "Now I know what got me here but I feel inadequate to change the tape that's playing in my brain."

One of my fellow nurses, Harriet Saxton, was planning to attend a weeklong School of Pastoral Care being conducted in a nearby city and invited me to be her roommate. Founded by Rev. Edgar Sanford, an Episcopal priest, and his wife, Agnes, the school provided teachings on Christian healing prayer for clergy and health care professionals.

Agnes Sanford's talks discussed what she termed "healing of memories." She shared her own story of several years spent struggling with severe clinical depression. Along with the depression, she had panic attacks which gripped her mind with fear regarding the safety of her husband and her children. A minister talked with her about her childhood and learned she had been raised in China by her parents who were missionaries. During the years spent in that country, she often heard the Chinese servants discussing the dangers of venturing outside the church compound. They graphically detailed the bandits who would rob and murder unsuspecting travelers. Each time Agnes' parents would leave the compound to preach the gospel she would experience extreme fear. She was certain they would never return.

As an adult she was exhibiting the same reactions when her husband and children left the house. The minister explained, "It isn't the adult woman who needs the prayers but the little girl who still lives within you." He prayed for Agnes, asking Jesus to go back in her life to those years in China and free her of the obsessive thoughts and feelings. Soon she began to notice a lifting of the veil that covered her mind. She never again experienced the darkness of depression.

This teaching gave me a piece of the puzzle missing from our work at the VA hospital. It wasn't enough to uncover the trauma that produced the behavior patterns expecting people to amend their performance. There needed to be a way to heal these old wounds. The healing power of Jesus provided that link.

Agnes told us she only knew two questions to ask people who felt they needed prayer for "healing of memories." The first was, "Were you happy when you were a little child?" If the person said, "No," she'd ask for the cause of the unhappiness. If the person said, "Yes," she would query, "When did you first notice you were unhappy?" She claimed the answers to these questions gave her adequate information to guide her prayers. After returning home, I was immediately presented with a situation that gave me an opportunity to use this method.

My neighbor, Delores, stopped by our house for one of her weekly visits. She was noticeably distraught as she described her life as a wife and mother. She felt overwhelmed by the things she had to do for her two children and her relationship with her husband was rapidly deteriorating. I was at a loss to offer any comfort when I remembered Agnes Sanford's teachings. So I asked her, "Delores, were you happy when you were a little girl?" At first she seemed surprised by this question but after a few minutes she quietly answered, "No." She then went on to relate an incident that occurred when she and her older sister were spending the summer on the farm with her aunt and uncle.

"We loved going there because we had lots of fun helping with the animals and riding on the tractor. But one very hot summer evening we left all the bedroom doors open in order to catch the hint of a breeze. My sister had gone to sleep but I was wide-awake as I listened to the conversation in the next room. My uncle stated, 'Isn't it a shame Delores isn't as bright and Betty?' My aunt agreed and added, 'She's also not as pretty. Life will be difficult for her.' They spoke at length about my faults. I knew they were right and I've spent my whole life feeling like a failure."

I told her about God's ability to heal the wounds of the past and asked her if I could pray for her to be freed from this debilitating memory. She doubted it would be helpful but told me to go ahead and try. I simply asked Jesus to walk back in time with Delores and remove the sorrow she experienced. She closed her eyes as I observed tears gently falling down her cheeks. She described the entire scene, right down to the color of her bedspread, the pattern of the wallpaper, and the curtains hanging at the window. She told me that Jesus was sitting on her bed and inviting her to come into his arms. "I accepted his invitation and listened as he told me how much I was loved. My heart was so happy to learn this truth about myself. I'll never again believe myself to be a failure."

The changes in Delores' life began immediately. She accepted a job as a waitress at a nearby country club and within months was managing the restaurant. Her relationships with husband and children were no longer a burden but became a source of much satisfaction. Once her attitude toward herself became healthier, others began to treat her with respect. Each year at Christmas I receive a card from her reminding me of the moment in time when Jesus set her free.

Our mutual experience set me on a mission to teach others about the awesome power of Jesus Christ in overcoming the pain of the past. Agnes Sanford used the term "healing of memories" to describe the power of Jesus Christ to transform negative emotions. However, I have found that term often causes confusion because people think it means their mind can be helped to remember things better! The older I get the more I understand why this could be an important form of restoration. So to avoid such misunderstandings I prefer to use the term "inner healing."

The basic idea of inner healing is simple: Jesus, "who is the same yesterday, today and forever" (Heb 13:8), can take the memories of our past and heal them from the wounds that effect our present life. In the process he fills our empty places and drains our hearts of the poison of resentment and hatred. Bringing God's light into the shadow areas of our inner self may be the most important step of our spiritual journey.

It's my hope that the message of this book will provide a source of renewal, healing, and enlightenment for all who seek wholeness and holiness.

—BARBARA SHLEMON RYAN, RN

CHAPTER ONE

WHAT IS INNER HEALING?

THE UNHEALED MEMORIES OF PSYCHOLOGICAL HURTS can exert a great deal of negative influence in our lives, keeping us from the emotional wholeness and holiness we so earnestly desire.

St. Paul recognized this important aspect of our psychological framework when he wrote a pastoral letter to the people of Ephesus. It included a prayer addressed to God which said in part; "Out of his infinite glory, may he give you the power through his Spirit for your *hidden self* to grow strong, so that Christ might live in your hearts" (Eph 3:16–17).

The Ephesians had accepted Jesus as their savior and been baptized in the Holy Spirit. They were recognized as a spiritually renewed group of early believers. Yet St. Paul was asking God to strengthen a hidden area within them so Jesus could be present on every level of their being. He further exhorts them, "You must give up your old way of life; you must put aside your old self, which gets corrupted by following illusory desires. Your mind must be renewed by a spiritual revolution so you can put on the new self that has been created in God's way" (Eph 4:22). He was identifying the shadow side of our nature, the unconscious part of our minds that often militates against our desire to be one with Christ.

Modern psychologists often use the image of an iceberg in describing the human mind. Like the part of the iceberg that is above the water, only a small portion of our mind, perhaps ten percent, is above the level of consciousness; only that portion is within our present awareness. It is impossible for us to remain fully conscious of every aspect of our lives, so the subconscious, which comprises 90 percent of the mind, is the repository for everything that has ever happened to us.

Good memories can usually be brought to consciousness without too much effort, but the traumatic episodes of our lives are often pushed deep into hidden recesses as we attempt to forget the experiences and the pain associated with them. Unfortunately, we cannot escape one of the characteristics of the unconscious; like an elephant, it *never forgets anything*. The unhealed hurts continue to fester within us, requiring large amounts of psychic energy and will power to contain them. Occasionally, when experiencing a period of unusual stress, we lose control of our ability to suppress all those feelings and we "overreact," "flip our lid," or "blow our cool." This terminology is beautifully descriptive of the mechanism involved. Something containing much energy has been released within us.

Unhealed hurts can sometimes lead to destructive behavior. For example, alcoholism, drug addiction, sexual promiscuity, gluttony, workaholism, or any form of addiction represent attempts to medicate the pain of the inner being. People are often unaware of the reason for constant tension in their lives, but they gradually develop habits to deal with it. Many psychosomatic illnesses can be attributed to the body's effort to resolve the problems of the mind.

It becomes obvious that the hurtful memories of the past cannot be ignored if we are to become filled with the love of the Father. The prayer of inner healing invites the power of Jesus Christ into the deep mind where he can effectively transform the painful memories from darkness into light. This transforming grace is freely accessible through the death and resurrection of the Lord. As Isaiah prophesied,

> Ours were the sufferings he bore,
>
> ours the sorrows he carried.
>
> But we, we thought of him as someone punished,
>
> struck by God, and brought low.
>
> Yet he was pierced through for our faults,
>
> crushed for our sins.
>
> On him lies a punishment that brings us peace,
>
> and through his wounds we are healed..
>
> —Isaiah 53:4–5

We are accustomed to equating the death of Jesus with forgiveness of the sins we have committed. But this passage clearly tells us that he also died for the sins committed against us. He bore our sufferings and carried our sorrows to the cross so that we would not have to bear such a heavy burden within us. His resurrected presence brought light into the darkness of the whole earth and, therefore, into the shadow areas of our minds.

Persons reared in families with constant mental and physical abuse, chronic illness or the death of a parent, alcoholism, or other disorders will have little trouble recognizing their need for healing prayer. But what about those from basically good families where the parents tried their best to care for them? Does everyone need some type of inner healing?

I am personally convinced that everyone is in some way bound by the chains of the past. We are born into a broken world and much of our suffering is due to the imperfections of those around us. No human being has ever been able to love us as completely as we desire.

Feelings of rejection, loneliness, and hurt are sometimes so subtle we fail to acknowledge their existence. Regardless of our recognition, these feelings are still capable of blocking emotional and spiritual growth.

Isn't faith in Jesus Christ sufficient to meet these inner needs? We do become spiritually healed when we accept him as the Lord and Savior of our life. Salvation and eternal life are secured through his death and resurrection. However, we can commit to the Lord only those parts of us that we are consciously recognize. The regions of the subconscious are below the level of our awareness and we do not always know what lies therein. The painful memories in the hidden self are often concealed, requiring an act of our will to invite the Lord to cleanse and set free those parts of our being.

Thus we can understand St. Paul's letter to the people of Ephesus. These Christians already knew Jesus Christ as Lord and Savior, yet there was more that needed to be done before they could be filled with his presence. The spirit needs to be free and the mind renewed before we can become the new creation God has called us to be.

Inner healing is a process. No single prayer, spiritual exercise, or meditative technique can possibly touch all the unhealed areas within us. The process of healing the inner person is a journey which we travel throughout our Christian lives as we gradually become infused with the light of God's love.

One of my favorite pastimes is raising roses in the garden and watching their beauty quietly unfold, one petal at a time, until they become glorious specimens of creation. If I were to try to force the petals open, the flowers would die, but with the proper application of sunlight, water, and food, they progress to become perfectly formed.

These same methods of patient gardening need to be applied to our inner being. There is an old poem illustrating the futility of trying to rush the process.

It is only a tiny rosebud,
A flower of God's design;
But I cannot unfold the petals
With these clumsy hands of mine.
The secret of unfolding flowers
Is not known to such as I.
God opens this flower so sweetly,
When in my hands they die.
If I cannot unfold a rosebud,
This flower of God's design,
Then how can I have the wisdom
To unfold this life of mine?
So I'll trust in Him for leading
Each moment of my day.
I will look to him for His guidance
Each step of the pilgrim way.
The pathway that lies before me,
Only my Heavenly Father knows.
I'll trust Him to unfold the moments,
Just as He unfolds the rose.

—Author Unknown

Our Father is a creator who touches each of us with unique and varied expressions of his love. Healing can come to us through many avenues of grace. The sacraments, music, poetry, scripture reading, and devotional literature may provide a mode of restoration. One woman related her experience in viewing the movie *The Turning Point*, a film depicting the relationship between two women who hold deep feelings of resentment and jealousy against each other. While watching the movie, my friend began to identify a similar situation in her own life; she confronted her need for healing and, subsequently, became reconciled with the other woman. God can utilize any means available to bring us into wholeness when we are willing to become conscious of our brokenness.

However, I believe most of us need some assistance in the beginning stages of the healing process and we cannot always find a priest, minister, therapist, or Christian friend who can pray the prayer of faith with us. Every day I receive messages from individuals desiring this type of ministry and, whenever possible, I refer them to a qualified person in their local area. Fortunately, the Association of Christian Therapists has been instrumental in teaching the principles of healing prayer to hundreds of health care professionals, thereby providing a growing network of Christian counseling centers throughout the United States. Nevertheless, no organization could possibly accommodate all the healing needs of today's world. This book endeavors to help alleviate the problem by providing some simple explanations and meditative prayers for those desiring inner healing.

Understanding that healing is a lifetime process that helps us to be patient with ourselves as we allow the love of Jesus Christ to gently bring us into the light.

Each of the following chapters will deal with a specific developmental stage in life, beginning with conception and proceeding through adulthood. A short explanation of the usual psychological problems encountered at each age level is presented with a meditative prayer to enable the reader to open his or her heart and mind to God's healing love. Obviously it would be impossible to confront every possible hindrance to growth on each level. This book is not meant to impart all knowledge on the subject of inner healing: it is meant to be only a facilitator for those who want to begin the process, but do not know how to start. It is written not merely to be read, but to be experienced.

Each person should seek to approach the various levels of inner healing at his or her own pace, recognizing that we have all been created as unique individuals and the Lord will deal differently with each of us. It may be best to spend several days or even weeks on the early stages of life—prenatal, birth, infancy—since these formative years have such a profound effect on our development. It is also advisable to utilize all the avenues of grace available to us through the sacraments, scripture reading, and church services.

Receiving the Eucharist for specific areas needing healing can be very helpful for members of churches which regularly provide Holy Communion. Each time Roman Catholics assist at the celebration of Mass, they approach the altar with the words, "Lord, I am not worthy to receive you, but only say the word and I shall be healed." Every Mass is really a healing service where we may receive the body and blood of Jesus to heal body, mind, and spirit. As we receive his resurrected body, therefore, we can invite him to heal those parts of us which are not yet filled with life in accordance with his teaching:

As I, who am sent by the living Father,

myself draw life from the Father

so whoever eats me will draw life from me.

—John 6:57

As we receive Jesus into ourselves, he is communicating his life to us very intimately and very deeply. We can ask him to bring life to our hidden selves, to brighten the shadowy recesses of our minds with the light of his love, and to give us the strength to continue to seek him in all our ways.

There are also many graces available to us through the forgiveness of our sins in the sacrament of reconciliation (confession). Members of the counseling profession have

often remarked to me that one of their biggest problems
is dealing with guilt, either real or imagined, in the lives or
their clients. The human spirit cries out for forgiveness
and cleansing:

> For I am well aware of my faults,
>
> I have my sin constantly in mind,
>
> having sinned against none other than you,
>
> having done what you regard as wrong.
>
> —Psalms 51:3

Dr. Karl Menninger, the famed psychiatrist and
founder of the Menninger Clinic in Topeka, Kansas, has
written a very successful book entitled *Whatever Became of
Sin?* in which he discusses the epidemic of violence in
today's world in the light of society's unwillingness to
admit corporate and personal sin. Dr. Menninger writes:

> The widespread need for open avowal and
> acknowledgement and confession (of sin)
> occasionally comes to light in the blooming of
> some new cult in which communication and
> disclosure are made part of self-realization. Such
> cults are often evanescent because they depend
> too much on superficial solutions, but they are
> popular because unconfessed guilt feelings are
> hard to bear. They must be confessed to someone!
>
> And the clergyman is a very special "someone."
> He stands in a special place; he has a special
> authority. Not just because he is "a man of
> God. . . ." If the minister says, "This is clearly
> sin," we usually accept that decision. Criminal
> or not, symptomatic or not, sinful he says it is,
> and the wages of sin are death. But there is
> a solution: penitence, confession, restitution,

atonement. Relief from a sense of guilt then begins automatically.

The human conscience is like the police: it may be eluded, stifled, drugged, or bribed. But not without cost.

No psychiatrist or psychotherapist, even those with many patients, has the quantitative opportunity to cure souls and mend minds which the preacher enjoys. And the preacher also has a superb opportunity to do what few psychiatrists can to prevent the development of chronic anxiety, depression, and other mental ills.

Many years ago Father Michael Scanlan wrote a small book entitled *The Power in Penance*, which profoundly affected the way in which many Roman Catholic priests administered the sacrament. In it he stated,

The history of the sacrament of penance records a strong tradition of confession as healing and therapeutic and as placing the priest in the role of "physician of the soul" and "spiritual doctor to heal wounds." This grew from the early church practice of confession as spiritual direction to a holy man, usually a monk, not necessarily a priest. The Church has continually taught that the sacrament provides healing and strengthening powers in the form of actual graces.

Father Scanlan presents an approach to the sacrament which enables the penitent to identify areas in his or her life which may be blocking or impeding the love of Jesus from flowing. Priest and penitent pray together, asking the Lord to reveal anything which needs to be removed in order that the process of life in God can flow more smoothly. Through

prayerful discernment and discussion the minister seeks to
help the penitent look beyond the current sin in order to
identify the basic problem which is often rooted in past
experiences of rejection and lack of love.

Along with these avenues of grace, regularly attending
church services and prayer meetings puts us in touch with
the Christian community and can be a valuable asset in
assisting the process of inner healing. Community worship
helps us to realize that we belong to a spiritual family
presided over by a heavenly Father who loves us more than
we can ever imagine. Learning to relate to our brothers and
sisters "in the Lord" can lend us the support we need in
our continuing effort to walk in the steps of Jesus.

It has been said that the longest journey in the world
begins with just one step. It is my prayer that the following
chapters will enable the reader to embark on the pilgrimage
which will bring the "life abundant" promised by the Lord.

A NOTE TO PARENTS

A word of caution is in order for parents who are
reading this book. It is a natural instinct to assess our own
child-rearing abilities when we read about situations from
conception to adolescence which can affect a person's
subsequent life. Because most parents are sincerely
attempting to provide their offspring with the very best
environment for growth, we experience guilt for our
shortcomings when we consider our imperfect parenting
skills.

The message of this book, however, is not meant to
bring condemnation but hope for all of us. As a parent of
five grown children, I am painfully aware of my areas of
inadequacy in meeting their psychological needs. However,
knowledge of inner healing has enabled me to ask Jesus
Christ to make up for any deficiencies demonstrated by
their father and me. Each day I intercede for our children,

asking Jesus to go back to those moments when we failed to show kindness, gentleness, and love. Occasionally I have prayed with one or another of our children for specific memories of trauma they suffered, but most often I simply lift them in prayer each day and trust in him to heal their emotional needs.

Frequently I encounter parents who express deep disappointment regarding the direction their children's lives have taken. Often they say, "We must have done something wrong in their upbringing." I remind them that even God didn't obtain perfect results from his children. The story of the garden of Eden in Genesis demonstrates the stubbornness of human nature when our first parents refused to obey the one rule given to them by Yahweh. Do we then assume that God was a bad parent in rearing his children or do we recognize that Adam and Eve were using their own free will in choosing to eat from the "tree of good and evil"?

Our heavenly Father never expected us to be perfect parents. If we did everything for our children, with no mistakes of any kind, then we would be "god" for them and they would never reach out to discover the true God for themselves. It's the empty, hurting areas within us which usually provide the impetus that finally draws us into the waiting arms of Jesus Christ who alone can supply all our needs.

So, as you are reading this book, if you become aware of ways in which you were not a source of life for your child, invite Jesus to touch those memories, receive his forgiveness for yourself, and release the situation into his care. The light that he gives us today is not to be directed back into our lives to burden us with condemnation but is to be a light "to guide our feet into the way of peace" (Lk 1:79).

CHAPTER TWO

PRENATAL

"WHY WOULD I NEED HEALING FOR THE TIME spent in my mother's womb? Before birth we are nothing but a blank slate," argued a gentleman who was attending one of our healing workshops. Until a few years ago it was commonly believed that John Locke's theory of the *tabula rasa* (blank slate) was correct. Infants supposedly entered the world as empty scrolls waiting for others to write on them.

Modern medicine, however, seems to be proving the error of this kind of thinking as researchers in dozens of laboratories and hospitals discover that infants in the womb are enormously complex. The fetus is clearly developing acute senses by the sixth month of gestation, according to pediatrician T. Barry Brazelton of the Children's Hospital Medical Center in Boston. When pregnant women (wearing abdominal belts to measure fetal response) enter rooms with bright lights and harsh noises, the fetuses are startled. In contrast, soft lights and sounds seem to soothe them.

In 1981, when psychiatrist Dr. Thomas Verney published his ground-breaking book, *The Secret Life of the Unborn Child*, he stunned the medical community by demonstrating that the unborn child is a feeling, remembering, aware being. What happens in the nine months between conception and birth molds and shapes the child's personality in very important ways. The old Freudian notion that personality doesn't begin to develop until the second or third year of life has forever been replaced by the pioneering work of the modern medical community.

Today's large volume of research data on fetal development has generated the formation of an International Society for the Study of Prenatal Psychology which deals with the continuity of fetal and postnatal life. This long-neglected area of human development is finally being given serious attention as psychologists are discovering its importance.

From the moment of conception, the brain develops more rapidly than at any other period of life, reaching three-quarters of its adult size by age two. This exceedingly rapid development of nerve pathways, it is believed, has a definite effect on a person's entire life and explains the importance of early experiences. Acute sensitivity causes negative situations to appear much worse than they are in reality, thus distorting the perception of these events and coloring the understanding of them. This is one reason why the prayer for inner healing can be so valuable. It relieves us of the faulty understanding of our past memories so we can obtain a better impression of the relationship between our parents and ourselves. This type of healing can also provide a better framework for relating to the presence of God in our lives as it opens us to receive more of his love.

Time and again I have prayed with persons plagued by feelings of fear, guilt, shame, or grief and have felt led by the Holy Spirit to ask Jesus to touch them during the time of their prenatal development. Occasionally individuals have recalled traumas their mothers experienced during pregnancy which caused the infant to absorb into itself the pain, grief, shame, or anger the mother was feeling. Sometimes they were made aware of these episodes because the mother or other family members passed on such information over the years. But, just as often, even though not consciously aware of any psychological trauma, their inner being felt a sense of release, comfort, and peace following the prayer. This liberation often enabled them to bring areas of their lives which had resisted integration into better order and balance.

Numerous books on the psychology of the prenatal period are appearing, many of them written by persons practicing various forms of hypnotism and re-birthing methods to elicit prenatal information. These techniques can be extremely risky because they do not provide the spiritual protection necessary when we attempt to enter the unconscious area of our being. In John's Gospel, Jesus tells us, "I am the gate. Anyone who enters through me will be safe; he will go freely in and out and be sure of finding pasture" (John 10:9). I interpret this to mean that the only safe way of entering the inner self is through the person of Jesus Christ under the power of the Holy Spirit. The Lord gently deals with our woundedness without the aid of drugs or exterior stimulation to generate a "cure."

The gentleman who expressed skepticism concerning healing prayer for the prenatal period discovered the answer to his question. During the afternoon workshop session, we led the group in a prayer meditation specifically for that period of time. In spite of his doubts, he was willing to enter into prayer "just in case it might be beneficial." He later described his experience:

> I felt Jesus leading me back in my life to the time before I was born and I became conscious of strong feelings of anger and resentment toward my mother, feelings I had never before recognized. As I asked Jesus to reveal the source of these emotions, I heard my mother's voice saying, "During my entire pregnancy with Danny,

I was hoping for a little girl." Suddenly I realized
that my mother's attitude constituted a rejection
from the very beginning of life. Small wonder I
had problems relating to women and was
confused about my sexuality. I asked the Lord to
heal this wound and immediately began to sense
waves of light washing over me. It seemed as if he
was saying, "It's all right for you to be a man." I
began to cry for the sheer joy of being able to
accept myself for the first time in my life.

This is but one example from the hundreds of
testimonies I have heard over the years. Such an experience
illuminates the words of Psalm 139:

It was you who created my inmost self,

and put me together in my mother's womb;

for all these mysteries I thank you:

for the wonder of myself, for the wonder of

your works.

—Psalms 139:13–14

The Lord is present to us during every phase of our
development and is capable of transforming any
psychological obstacle into a source of new life.

Sometimes we may even need healing for the very first
moment of our life on earth, the moment of conception. I
have absolutely no doubts that life begins with the
penetration of sperm into ovum, having prayed for
numerous individuals whose emotional problems were
greatly reduced when we asked Jesus to heal them of any
negativeness associated with their conception, such as
illegitimacy or rape.

Any threat to life during gestation, it seems, can cause
anxiety and fear to cling to a person throughout life.
For example, a possibility of miscarriage and the mother's

fear of losing a baby could cause the infant to receive the message of "fear of death" and to suffer from this anxiety as an adult. Therapy can uncover the fear, but the healing love of Jesus Christ is usually necessary to obtain complete release.

One of my first experiences in praying this type of prayer involved the adopted baby of neighborhood friends. The mother noted that the infant boy did not respond in a normal way to touching and holding, assuming a rigid posture with tightly closed fists most of the time. He had much difficulty retaining formula and, by the age of three weeks, was exhibiting serious digestive problems resulting in hospitalization. The parents asked me to pray with him after a diagnosis of pyloric stenosis (closure of the valve opening into the stomach) was confirmed by X-ray and surgery was contemplated.

As I laid hands on the child, the tension in his body was very obvious and I asked the Lord to heal him of his physical symptoms. I felt the Holy Spirit guiding me to pray for him during the prenatal period, especially for the fear and guilt experienced by his natural mother. The only information we had concerning her was that she was unmarried, so it was reasonable to suspect a high degree of anxiety during the pregnancy. As I asked Jesus to release the baby of the ways in which he was wounded by his mother's pain, he began to relax and sleep peacefully. The surgery was canceled when he was able to retain feedings and the mother reported a dramatic difference in his ability to respond to affection.

Often I have prayed with persons whose mothers attempted to abort them. Whether or not they were consciously aware of their mothers' actions, they felt throughout their lives a barrier in the mother/child relationship, a lack of trust or irrational fear of the mother.

Beverly told me she was overwhelmed by feelings of guilt over her attempt to abort her child in the early stages of her pregnancy. Her husband divorced her when he learned she was expecting a baby and she felt abandoned by everyone. "One day I decided to throw myself down a flight of stairs in an effort to produce a miscarriage," she explained. "However, as I stood at the head of the stairs, I suddenly felt that everything would be all right if I'd just trust in God. Several months later I delivered a healthy baby girl, but all these years I've struggled to forgive myself for even thinking of losing her. She's a grown woman now and we don't have the close relationship that a mother and daughter should have." Over the years, Beverly had received absolution in the sacrament of reconciliation but this hadn't alleviated her feelings of shame.

I prayed with her, asking Jesus to take her back to the time of her early pregnancy. We ask the Lord to relieve her distress and remove the negative emotions associated with the pregnancy. She "saw" herself standing at the top of the stairs. But, this time she was aware of Jesus' presence. She understood it was the voice of God telling her to trust. She wept as she accepted his healing touch as the old feelings melted from her heart.

Several weeks later, she called to tell me that her daughter was coming for a visit. She felt some anxiety because on previous occasions there had been much tension between them. We prayed together for a peace-filled time of renewal and the prayer was answered in a wonderful moment of grace. Her daughter told her that she frequently suffered from nightmares which gripped her with feelings of terror. She said, "I see myself falling down a flight of stairs into a pit of darkness. It seems I am going to be swallowed up." Beverly then shared her experience of desperation during the pregnancy and, together, they prayed for her daughter to be freed. The nightmare never recurred and mother and daughter established a more open relationship.

The fetus, it seems, is also extremely sensitive to feelings of the father and "picks up" his responses during the gestation period. If the father welcomes this new life and anticipates the birth, the infant feels secure and protected. But if he rejects mother and/or infant, it can lead to a sense of worthlessness, constant feelings of inferiority, and lack of self-esteem.

Research done in Finland showed that the absence of a father during the prenatal period can cause psychological problems in later life. An index group of persons whose fathers had died before they were born was compared to a control group whose fathers had died during the first year of their lives. (Most of the fathers had been killed in World War II.) When the groups were evaluated, psychiatric and behavioral disorders were more than twice as common in the index group, showing a strong correlation between the father's emotional support during the prenatal time and the emotional well-being of the mother and child.

Any violence, such as physical or verbal abuse, directed to the mother during pregnancy is likely to be accepted by the child as also meant for it since the infant perceives no separation between self and the mother.

A Christian counselor told of praying with a woman whose father, an alcoholic, regularly beat the mother and children during long periods of drunkenness. The woman grew up in this atmosphere of hostility, marrying at an early age to escape from home. As is often the case, the man she married was also abusive and it became increasingly evident that she had to separate from him before he killed her. Many hours of counseling and prayer were required over a period of months before she became strong enough to take that step. "The breakthrough came when we prayed for her during the time she spent in the womb," he said. "As we asked Jesus to surround her with his protective love and to stand between the pregnant mother and the violent father, she became aware that the Lord was receiving the blows in place of her mother. The scripture 'through his wounds we are healed' leaped into her mind. She became aware that Jesus allowed himself to be physically beaten during his passion so that she could be set free. It was an extraordinary moment of grace which brought her much peace."

The human spirit, it would seem, is supersensitive to the attitudes and feelings of others. The fetus developing within the mother is not a mere collection of protoplasm, but an exceptionally impressionable form of life. How else can we explain the scriptural narrative of Mary, the mother of Jesus, and the visit to her cousin, Elizabeth? Mary is in the very early stages of pregnancy, probably the first few weeks, while Elizabeth is in her sixth month. Nevertheless, the infant John the Baptist is capable of recognizing and responding to the presence of the Lord.

> Now as soon as Elizabeth heard Mary's greeting, the child leapt in her womb and Elizabeth was filled with the Holy Spirit. She gave a loud cry and said, "Of all women you are the most blessed, and blessed is the fruit of your womb. Why should I be honored with a visit from the mother of my Lord? For the moment your greeting reached my ears, the child in my womb leapt for joy"
>
> —Luke 1:41-44

Elizabeth's interpretation of her baby's action may seem a bit simplistic to our present-day mentality, yet the fact remains that she had no outwardly discernible way of knowing Mary's condition except through the divine revelation precipitated by John's behavior. These two infants in utero were, in a sense, communicating with one another.

Sometimes the prenatal period of our lives can be surrounded by so much darkness that it severely affects our life. On several occasions I've felt led to pray for a person to be removed from the toxicity of their mother's womb and placed into the safe environment of our mother Mary's womb. One such situation involved a mother who was psychotic and confined to a mental hospital during her pregnancy. The infant born to her was adopted by a kind and loving family but the child experienced deep depression during most of her life. Each time she received the Eucharist, I encouraged her to "imagine" herself within the protection of Mary's body. Within a few weeks, she was freed of inner darkness and never again experienced what she termed "black pit depression."

This sensitivity to the world around us can bring blessings as well as pain during the prenatal period. Because I have been focusing attention on the *problems* encountered during the gestation period, it may seem as if this portion of our lives is filled with nothing but negativity. I want to emphasize, therefore, that most of us were born to parents who affirmed us and loved us as they anticipated our births. The deep mind holds countless memories of positive encounters with those who cared for us during the early years of our lives. As our deep mind is relieved of the hurtful remembrances, we can begin to touch the more creative aspects of our being. It would be a mistake for an expectant couple to begin to fear that any tension in their relationship would produce irreparable damage to their unborn child. A certain amount of tension is always present within us and concentrating energy to completely eradicate it only creates more anxiety. Knowing that we can call upon the healing love of Jesus Christ to strengthen this hidden portion of ourselves relieves us of the burden of perfection in this regard.

The following prayer is intended to begin the process of freeing those areas which felt insufficiently affirmed and loved. It is not necessary that we be consciously aware of such woundedness; the light of God's love will search the hidden self to discover any unhealed areas as we yield to his loving touch.

LORD JESUS CHRIST, I ask you to lead me back to the very beginning of my life on this earth. Through the power of your Holy Spirit guide me to that moment in time when I was created through the physical union of my father and mother.

Touch my parents with your perfect love and supply whatever may have been lacking in their union with one another so my conception may be surrounded with a positive, affirming environment of healing light.

As the components of my life become fused, release me from anything genetically harmful so my body can grow strong and healthy. Set me free from inherited psychological traits which could affect the development of my mind. Touch my spirit to wash clean any unholiness in my family background that might impede my ability to walk with Jesus Christ.

"You know me through and through from having watched my bones take shape when I was being formed in secret, knitted together in the limbo of the womb . . ." (Ps 139). You know the ways in which I need your loving touch upon this portion of my existence. Shine your light upon me to bring freedom and peace.

Lord, I do praise and thank you for all the beautiful ways I was loved and affirmed during my growth within my mother. I am grateful for the parents you

gave me and ask you to help me forgive them for
the times when I did not perceive their love.

Encircle me with a blanket of your protective light
to deflect any negativity which may have come
upon me from feelings of sorrow, anger, guilt, fear, or
shame which could have crossed the placental barrier
and entered into me.

Let this stage of my life be surrounded with such
warmth that I will eagerly anticipate my impending
birth. Dispel any dark fears for my safety; release
any anxieties concerning my physical condition.
Help me to believe that you will never permit me to
face trials without your love to sustain me as I recall
your promise to remain with us always.

I place this area of my life in the care of Jesus Christ,
believing that you will accomplish any needed
healing in your way and in your time. AMEN.

CHAPTER THREE

BIRTH

CHILDBIRTH IS AN AWESOMELY BREATHTAKING moment when mother, father, and those in attendance profoundly experience the creative power of God. As a delivery room nurse for ten years, I was privileged to assist in numerous deliveries, always with the overwhelming feeling of wonder that such an intricate human baby could be so perfectly developed in 280 days.

Giving birth to our five children reinforced these feelings as my husband and I would hold each newborn infant and thank God for this special gift to us. Indeed, the arrival of a new baby is usually a time for much congratulating and receiving cards and presents.

With all this rejoicing, why should the time of birth need healing prayer? Because the infant inspiring all this joyful activity has just come through one of the most harrowing episodes of its life and, on the whole, we are completely oblivious to the trauma. We are aware of the mother's labor pains and her postpartum discomforts, but only in recent years have we begun to explore the newborn's response to the process of birth.

It was the work of a French obstetrician, Dr. Frederick Leboyer, which first focused medical attention on the plight of the infant during childbirth. His book, *Birth Without Violence*, evoked rather dramatic changes in many delivery rooms as physicians and nurses became more sensitive to the baby's needs. Dr. Leboyer states, "What makes being born so frightful is the intensity, the boundless scope and variety of the experience, its suffocating richness. People say, and believe, that a newborn baby feels nothing. He feels everything. Everything without choice or filter or discrimination. Birth is a tidal wave of sensation, surpassing anything we can imagine. A sensory experience so vast we can barely conceive of it."

Leboyer has delivered more than 10,000 babies, the last 1,000 brought into the world by a new method of gentleness and consideration which he developed. Since the fetus in the womb has not been subjected to loud noises and bright lights, Dr. Leboyer reduces the delivery room illumination to the barest minimum and requires total silence (except for absolutely necessary directions given in the lowest possible whisper).

Immediately after birth, the infant, still attached to the placenta, is placed on the mother's abdomen in order to preserve the intimacy between mother and child. There the baby is gently stroked and permitted to breathe according to its own timetable. The spine, which has been curved in the fetal position for nine months, is not suddenly jerked straight as the baby is held upside down and "spanked" to encourage breathing. With much patience and understanding on the part of the delivery room team, the newborn is gradually enabled to become separated from the protective environment of the uterus. The more frightening aspects of the birth procedure have been lessened considerably.

Do these precautionary measures produce any improvements in the infant's subsequent development? Thousands of hours of research have proved the effectiveness of gentle birthing techniques. One study conducted by psychologist Danielle Rapaport at the French Science Council compared 120 one-, two-, and three-year-olds delivered by the Leboyer technique and a similar number delivered in conventional ways. She tested the children for motor skills, language ability, and general development. The two groups began to speak at the same age, on the average, but the Leboyer children walked earlier and did considerably better in psychomotor development.

In *The Birth Book*, one couple detailed the marked difference in their experiences after birthing eight children. "We have found that many couples see birth as an ordeal to be survived. They don't realize that birth can be satisfying and enjoyable. When it's a positive and enriching event, life with baby gets off to a better start. Birthing matters."

These studies do seem to indicate something beneficial is being derived from this system. Dr. Nathan Hirsch, who delivers babies by the Leboyer method in the Miami area, states that he considers it an excellent means of birth. "It doesn't make a better baby, but it makes a better family unit, especially at a stressful time (birth), and it may make the mother try harder to continue gentle ways," he said. In 1968, psychologist Deborah Tanzer became the first person to study the effects of the father's participation in childbirth. She discovered that bringing the father into the birth process in explicit ways, such as bathing and touching the infant, allows him to experience an immediate rapport with this new life. This early bonding can create a high degree of security for the whole family since it frequently strengthens marriages.

In their book, *A Good Birth, A Safe Birth*, Diane Korte and Roberta Scaer describe research done on the 1970s when more than 2000 women in the United States responded to a questionnaire regarding childbirth. All asked for the experience to become more gentle and humane. They felt hospital maternity options needed to allow for greater participation by the birth father, less noise and confusion in the birthing room, and permission for the infant to remain with the mother.

Much has been written about the importance of "bonding" in the early stages of life. This term implies unity, fusion, a coming together—a phenomenon which occurs first of all through the sense of touch. A baby has an acute ability to feel sensation through the skin. During gestation it is surrounded with the amniotic fluid which cushions it from sudden shocks. At birth the skin is completely covered with a thick coating of a white, pasty substance known as *vernix caseosa* to protect its sensitivity. Therefore gentle touching and stroking in this early stage of life enables the infant to begin to trust those who are caring for it. Throughout the remainder of our existence on earth we continue to need periodic doses of touching and hugging to assure us that we belong. Perhaps that is one of the reasons Jesus so frequently touched those around him while he walked among us during his earthly ministry. He recognized the value of tactile sensation as he laid his hands upon the sick and taught his disciples to do the same.

Drs. Marshall Klaus and John Kennell, two pediatricians at Rainbow Babies and Children's Hospital in Cleveland, Ohio, have done a considerable amount of research on the importance of early contact between parent and child. In one carefully controlled experiment where they compared mothers who had hours of intimate contact with other mothers who had only brief encounters, they found that a month after birth mothers who had more early contact with their babies were noticeably more affectionate, i.e., they gazed into their eyes and caressed their children with greater frequency, than the other mothers. At one year, they were observed in the doctor's office touching their children with soothing gestures more often than the other mothers, and by the time their children were two years of age they spoke to them with a greater number of words using fewer commands than did the other mothers. Dr. Kennell concludes that the studies indicate "the earlier you put mother and child together for extended periods, the more powerful the effects will be."

Currently there are mountainous amounts of research materials being published on the effects of the birth process and the first few hours of life on future psychological and physical development.

A mother living in Ontario, Canada, related the following story to me.

> For several years our ten-year-old son, Nick, has expressed fear and concern before falling asleep at night. He would usually say, "Mom, I'm having these scary thoughts again." His father and I would always pray for him asking God for good dreams or thoughts to replace any scary thoughts and cover him with protection through the night. Nick always found the transition into sleeping a challenge and was insistent that we pray for him.
>
> There was a common theme to these thoughts. He expressed fear of someone breaking into the house, bad people breaking in and hurting him. The consistency of these thoughts puzzled and concerned me. I didn't think he was just imaging things as this isn't part of his personality. It didn't seem connected to outside influences, such as TV or movies. There was something very real about his concerns and I began fearing that someone had broken into our home at night and abused the children without our knowledge.
>
> One night, as I was praying with the children at bedtime, Nick again said, "Mom, I'm having those scary thoughts again." I asked him to tell me once more about these feelings as I silently prayed for God to give me wisdom for my son. He again shared his fear of bad people breaking in to his house and God immediately gave me the revelation that these thoughts were directly

related to his birth experience. I had never considered this connection before and hadn't read of this anywhere, but I just knew God was showing this to me.

When Nick was born, he nearly bled to death before birth. The cord had broken away from the placenta while I was in early labor requiring an emergency C-section to save his life. It couldn't have happened more quickly. He was delivered in ten minutes time from when I began bleeding and the baby had no vital signs. It took very invasive and abusive procedures to save his life. Everything surrounding his birth was definitely a miracle, including his complete recovery in only ten days and his normal development since.

But, as I prayed, God showed me how damaging and frightening this birth experience was for Nick and, although his mind couldn't recall it, his spirit did. His birth experience was very much like a "breaking and entering" when his safe place was quickly torn apart and he immediately experienced a lot of seemingly bad things required to save his life.

As God revealed this, I knew he needed prayer. I wondered who I could ask to pray with Nick, someone who *really* knew how to pray for such things. I realized I would have to do for now. I shared my thoughts about his birth experience with Nick and we prayed a short, simple prayer asking God to bring healing to his birth memories and remove his fears of bad people breaking in. It was short, but specific, and not with a whole lot of faith. I was still thinking that this would be a stop-gap prayer until "real" prayers could be said at a later date.

God, however, does hear a mother's prayers for her child!

Since that night Nick has never had another scary thought at bedtime. We have definitely noticed a more settled and peaceful spirit about him. Each of us is complete; our past and our words are known to him. He really does desire to heal our hearts.

My experiences in prayer for inner healing have convinced me that most of us require some release from pain and trauma associated with our births. Even the most ideal circumstances cannot completely abolish anxiety and fear from the delivery process since the infant appears to be aware of much that is happening at that time. The March 1981 newsletter published by the International Childbirth Education Association narrates two conversations between mothers and their two-year-olds. In the first conversation, Linda Mathison was bathing her son Todd when she questioned him:

Mother: Todd, do you remember what it was like to be born, when you came out?

Todd: I went down the tunnel.

Mother: What did it feel like?

Todd: Like exercise.

Mother: What happened then?

Todd: 1-2-3-4-5-6-7-8-9-10.

Mother: What was it like when you left the tunnel?

Todd: Light.

Mother: It was light. Was there anything else?

Todd: It was cold!

Mother: Where were you before you were born, Todd?

Todd: In a light bulb. It broke!

In a later conversation, Todd explained that before he was born he was in a warm pond sleeping on a "baby thing," and he described being scared of the "lightning."

Another mother, Mary Cunniffe-Holtz, related an incident which occurred when she and her two-year-old son Gregory were looking through a Kodak viewer, one which uses a circular picture card. The viewer, when empty, revealed to Gregory's eye a dark tunnel with a dim light at the end. Three weeks prior to this moment, Gregory had asked his mother where he came from and she answered, "You were inside me. You were in my uterus, then you came out of my vagina." There followed no discussion of birthing.

After Greg looked into the empty viewer, he gazed up at his mother and, in a tone not at all surprised, began to speak. "Oh look, Mom, I'm coming through your vagina. I'm being born."

Mother: What does it feel like, Greg?

Greg: It's too tight!

Mother: What do you see?

Greg: The light is too bright! Everybody has white coats on. Daddy has white on, too.

After having these conversations, both children forgot what happened. At age four, neither, when asked, recalled anything about birth. When I shared this information with my co-worker, Diane Brown, she tested out the same questions with her three-year-old granddaughter, Alisha, with similarly fascinating results. Perhaps if we listened more intently to the "imaginative" discourses of the young, we might discover the rich storehouse of remembrances carried within all human hearts.

As noted previously, psychologists believe that the unconscious mind never forgets anything that has occurred in a person's life and, although we may consciously have no recollection of being born, the memory is still retained within us. Numerous times I have prayed for persons to be healed of any trauma associated with their birth and they have envisioned the whole scene as it was brought to their minds. Occasionally they described feelings of pressure over their bodies as they sensed being conveyed through the birth canal, experiencing momentary fear at the prospect of being born.

I wish to emphasize the fact that it is not necessary to relive the birth experience in order for healing to take place. In fact, sometimes displays of emotionalism in response to inner healing prayer are a deterrent to the process, focusing attention on feelings rather than the inner working of the healing power of God. Some current forms of therapy, such as Primal Therapy, require a person to re-experience every detail of the birth process with appropriate expression of feelings before psychological release can be accomplished. The Holy Spirit is a two-edged sword; with one side he reveals our need for healing and, almost simultaneously, he heals our painful memories. Our reaction to this revelation may be tears, but this is not essential. Healing occurs because we yield and are open to the Lord's touch as he replaces the pain with a sense of peace and well being.

One woman related the following experience:

During our prayer time, as you asked Jesus to take me back to the moment of my birth, I was aware of a high degree of fear. There seemed to be much tension in the air around me with people shouting in loud voices. It was always a joke in my family that I couldn't wait to be born and my mother delivered me in the back seat of the car as Daddy was racing to the hospital.

Reliving the scene in my imagination enabled me to understand why I never thought it was such a laughing matter. Daddy's voice was angry, telling Mom to stop making so much noise and she better not have that baby in his car. Mom was crying hysterically and screaming, "I can't help it, she's coming," as I emerged. My feeling was of overwhelming guilt. I had done something which brought disapproval from my parents and it was all my fault.

Maybe this has something to do with a feeling of not belonging which has always seemed to be with me. I asked Jesus to heal me of these memories and felt an immediate release of tension. It was like warm water being poured over me to wash away my guilt. I know this healing is somehow affecting my attitude about myself, because recently my sister made a remark about my "speedy" entry into the world and I could laugh about it for the first time.

Many persons have not experienced such dramatic birth situations, yet the need for healing prayer may still remain. Entry into the world, even in the best of conditions, contains elements of tension and fear which can subtly impede our psychological growth. Any departure from the normal process, i.e., use of forceps,

Caesarean section, breech presentation, premature delivery, multiple births, prolonged labor, etc., usually indicates an area which may need to be healed. Since Jesus Christ is the same yesterday, today, and forever, we can invite him to relieve the negativity associated with our birth process, thereby enabling us to embrace the true joy of the gift of life.

It is interesting to note the numerous times Jesus mentions the word "life" in his teachings. The gospel of John records thirty-four occasions when Jesus tells us that true life can be experienced only in him. For example,

It is the spirit that gives life,

the flesh has nothing to offer.

The words I have spoken to you are spirit

and they are life.

—John 6:63

Again, in the beautiful passage where he describes himself as the Good Shepherd, Jesus tells us,

I have come

so that they may have life

and *have it to the full*.

—John 10:10, italics added

As we enter into this prayer for healing, let us ask the Lord to release us of any impediments to living life to the full.

DEAR JESUS, I ask you to go back with me to that moment in time when the process of birth first began in my life. Please relieve me of any apprehensions I may have felt as the contractions of labor interrupted the serenity and calm of the womb forcing me into the birth canal.

Lord, let the gentleness of your touch quiet my fears, reassuring me that you will see me safely through this dark tunnel.

Jesus, I ask you to heal me of any complications associated with my birth. If it was necessary for the physician to apply forceps, perform a Caesarean section, correct an improper presentation, or use any type of extraordinary methods in my delivery, please release me of any negative effect this may have had on my development. Give me the grace to be able to entrust myself completely into your care by accepting the gift of life you gave to me through my parents by saying, "Yes, Lord, I want to be born. I desire to come to life."

Jesus, wash away any sense of guilt I may be carrying in regard to the pain and suffering my mother experienced in bringing me to birth. If my mother endured any untoward physical or psychological trauma as a result of my birth or if complications of the delivery caused her death, please set me free from the burden of responsibility for this situation which weighs so heavily upon me. Enable me to receive your forgiveness, to wash

away these guilty feelings, thereby allowing me to
forgive myself and accept myself more completely.

Jesus, I believe that you were present at the moment
of my birth for you told the disciples, "Know that I
am with you always; yes, to the end of time" (Mt
28:20). Therefore, as I emerged from the darkness
of the womb and into the light of the world, I ask
you to receive me into your arms, hold me close to
your heart, and fill me with courage and confidence
in facing the perils of the world. Help me to trust in
your protective love to surround me during times of
crisis and pain just as the scripture promises:

Does a woman forget her baby at the breast,
or fail to cherish the son of her womb?
Yet even if these forget,
I will never forget you.
See, I have branded you on the palms of my hands.
                    —Isaiah 49:15–16, italics added

Jesus, breathe your breath, your Spirit, into my
lungs, so that my first moment of life is blessed
with your life. Release me from any fear of death or
abnormal concern for my health which may have
entered into me as a result of problems with
resuscitation, prematurity, or other complications.
Allow me to experience a new joy and freedom
surrounding the gift of life being given to me by
God through my parents.

I thank you for the mother and father who brought
me into existence and ask you to bless them in a

special way today. As I meditate on the time of my birth, I ask Jesus to gently place me into the arms of my mother. Unite us in a firm bond of love which will enable me to feel secure in her acceptance of me. Supply any deficit of love between us with your perfect love.

In the same way, I ask you to put me into the arms of my father that I might experience his acceptance of me as his child. Heal me of any sense of rejection or disapproval which I may have perceived and surround us with your total affirmation of my being.

Heavenly Father,

It was you who created my inmost self,

and put me together in my mother's womb;

for all these mysteries I thank you:

for the wonder of myself, for the wonder
of your works.
> —Psalms 139:13–14

I give praise for the ways in which you are healing me of the darkness associated with my birth so that I may truly enter into the wonder and the beauty of life. AMEN.

CHAPTER FOUR

INFANCY

T HE MEDIEVAL WRITER SALIMBENE TELLS OF AN experiment conducted by Frederick II, Holy Roman emperor and king of Sicily in the thirteenth century. According to Salimbene, whose reflections were collected by historian C.G. Coulton, Frederick's heartless experiments included this one on the emotional needs of infants:

> He wanted to find out what kinds of speech and what manner of speech children would have when they grew up if they spoke to no one beforehand. So he bade foster mothers and nurses to suckle the children, to bathe and wash them but in no way to prattle with them or speak to them for he wanted to learn whether they would speak the Hebrew language, which was the oldest, or the Greek or Latin or Arabic, or perhaps the language of their parents of whom they had been born. But he labored in vain, because the children all died. For they could not live without the petting and joyful faces and loving words of their foster mothers.

Seven hundred years later, a whole series of studies of children raised in institutions "without the petting and joyful faces and loving words" of their mothers or foster mothers confirms the conclusions of this ancient chronicler. As late as the second decade of the twentieth century, the death rate for infants under one year of age in various foundling institutions throughout the United States was nearly 100 percent!

It was in 1915 that Dr. Henry Dwight Chapin, the distinguished New York pediatrician, in a report on children's institutions in ten different cities, made the staggering disclosure that in all but one institution every infant under two years of age died. The mortality rate in one foundling home was so high that it was customary to enter the condition of every infant on the admission card as hopeless.

In his informative book on the importance of touching, anthropologist Ashley Montague describes the work of Boston physician Dr. Fritz Talbot, who introduced the practice of tender, loving care to American nurseries. While in Germany during World War I, Dr. Talbot visited the Children's Clinic in Dusseldorf. He noted that the wards were neat and tidy, but his curiosity was piqued at the sight of a fat old woman carrying a baby on her hip. When he inquired about her, the director replied, "That's Old Anna. When we have done everything we can medically for a baby and it is still not doing well, we turn it over to Old Anna and she's always successful."

Dr. Talbot was presented with a very difficult task in bringing this simple solution into American institutions because the country was under the strong influence of the teachings espoused by a Dr. Luther Holt in his booklet, *The Care and Feeding of Children.* Holt, a professor of pediatrics at Columbia University, recommended such practices as the abolition of the cradle, not picking up the baby when it cried, feeding it by the clock, and not spoiling it with much handling.

These methods of child care were not completely discounted until after the Second World War when studies proved that applications of "mother love" brought about dramatic results with babies who refused to eat and were dying of starvation. The condition of these babies, known as marasmus, from the Greek word meaning "wasting away," was responsible for the majority of infant deaths. At Bellevue Hospital in New York, the mortality rate for infants under one year fell from 35 percent to less than 10 percent after orders were given that every baby should be picked up, carried around, and "mothered" several times a day.

Ashley Montague writes,

> What the child requires if it is to prosper . . . is to be handled, and carried, and caressed, and cuddled and cooed to . . . for it would seem that even in the absence of a great deal else, these are the reassuringly basic experiences the infant must enjoy if it is to survive in some semblance of health.

Dr. T. Berry Brazelton, chief of the Child Development Unit at Boston's Children's Hospital, focused attention on this subject in the overflowing orphanages of Cambodia in the 1970s, where the Thai border holding camps alone contained more than 3,500 children. Each of the older orphan girls there was assigned to care for four or five babies under the age of two. Since the girls were also survivors of the horrors of war, they had very little to give their tiny charges. At best, they carried a favorite baby around on their hip all day.

On a visit to the camps Dr. Brazelton observed that,

> I found that I could stand at the doorway of a baby room and pick out the infants who were favorites. When I called out across a room, it was the alert favorite who looked at me. He or she alone smiled and crooned . . . the rest of the babies were too depressed, too inexperienced in the loving give-and-take that does so much for normal

development. They lay on their backs all day, and the hair was worn off the back of their heads. They had been salvaged physically. They lived. But the quality of their lives, now and in the future, certainly is in question. We recently learned from working in developing countries, that children who are both malnourished and don't have a stimulating environment during infancy are unteachable by the time they reach first grade.

All these research studies appear to arrive at the same conclusion: A child's basis for emotional sturdiness is formed during early infancy. Most of the data demonstrates that the love and affection a child receives from the mother and father or other consistent care-giver from its birth through age three will determine the path of emotional development which will carry it through life.

During the years I worked in obstetrical nursing, new mothers would often ask for advice on baby care. I was very enthusiastic in encouraging breast feeding if possible and teaching them always to be certain to hold the baby while feeding regardless of the method. While I still feel strongly about this advice, I would now also counsel the importance of "petting" (touching), the "joyful faces" (sights), and the "loving words" (sounds), together with the smells and the tastes that are the necessary requirements for healthy infancy.

It is the singing, the smiling at one another, the nonsense talk, the rocking, and all the silly behavior between parent and child which truly constitute "love and affection." These types of interactions should be performed by both mother and father to provide a rich source of social stimuli for the child.

Sigmund Freud tended to believe that the baby's attachment to the mother was based on her being the source of gratification in terms of nourishment. However, John Bowlby, a British psychiatrist, believes that there is a deep instinct on the part of infants to attach themselves to one figure, to differentiate between that figure and all others, and the figure is more likely to be the "joyful face" than the provider of nourishment in cases where the two are not the same. In the Israeli kibbutz, for example, where the provider of food and the mother are usually not the same, the mother is nevertheless the principal attachment figure.

The importance of the interaction between parents and the baby cannot be overemphasized. Dr. Brazelton explained to the caregivers in the Cambodian orphanages how to play and talk to the babies. They were astounded to see one infant's "worried, old-man look" replaced by an alert listening as the doctor played with him. "One ten-month-old delighted the entire staff by imitating me after I scribbled with my pen on a piece of paper," he said. "They couldn't believe that 'just a baby' could be so alive and responsive."

As mentioned in the previous chapter, infants are not passive organisms but complex and intricate human beings who are extremely sensitive to the world around them. They appear to be acutely aware of the emotional climate in the home and to react with appropriate responses. I recall being angry about a broken washing machine as I was caring for our infant son, Chris, when he was a few weeks old. The dirty diapers and baby clothing (this was before the discovery of Pampers) were accumulating in piles throughout our apartment, lending a less than aromatic environment to my already nasty mood. In the midst of trying to discuss the situation with our landlady, the baby awoke and immediately began to scream his lungs out. No amount of attention eased his cries until a friend dropped by for a visit, picked him up, and he promptly fell asleep. That experience was the first of many encounters in the rearing of our children which taught me the reality of infant sensitivity to the feelings of others.

Of course, there are many instances when a baby is irritable and fretful without being antagonized by external stimuli, but that does not give us license to totally ignore parental responsibility in this area. I once heard a speaker muse that it is commonplace for a child of three or four to pick up a foreign language if exposed to it without any formal teaching. Yet we are unwilling to admit that a child of the same age picks up our unconscious attitudes and prejudices without being taught—and often retains these longer than any of his formal education. Learning how to create an environment of healthy interaction between parent and child can be of great value in subsequent stages of life.

Ministering prayer for inner healing has provided me with a rich opportunity to pray with hundreds of individuals. Very often I have felt led to intercede for the period of infancy and early childhood with special emphasis on healing faults in the parent-child relationship. The real or perceived memories of being neglected, abused, abandoned, or rejected can have a very definite effect on our ability to adjust to the myriad demands of life. Again, it is imperative to repeat a characteristic of the human mind: we magnify the negative input, while tending to ignore positive memories, because the former speak so loudly within us. The emotions associated with fear, pain, and anger manifest such strong impulses within our nervous system that they become permanently engraved in our unconscious mind. However, the gentle remembrances of joy, love, peace, and warmth do not produce such overwhelming responses and are therefore not recorded with such defined emphasis.

Nevertheless, every event which touches our lives remains somewhere within us even though we may have lost touch with it long ago. Neurologists have demonstrated this truth by stimulating long-repressed memories of patients under a local anesthetic by touching areas of the brain with tiny electric currents. Such arousal of buried memories often allows the patient to describe the past scene in intricate detail, down to the color and pattern of the rug and the smells wafting from the kitchen.

I have come to appreciate the value of inner healing prayer in its ability to free us from the burden of painful situations so we can concentrate more of our energies on recognizing the beauty within ourselves.

One example is a priest who experienced his first encounter with inner healing prayer on a visit to my home. He asked me to pray with him concerning a problem in his parish, but during our conversation it became obvious to me that there were deeper needs in his life.

My inquiries about his childhood were met with noticeable irritability since he was intent on solving the problems "current" to his priesthood. I persisted, however, until he finally gave me a sketchy account of his background. The information became significant with his first sentence, "I guess I should begin by telling you that I'm adopted." Whatever else he shared became only background as I listened to the guidance of the Holy Spirit within me and realized his great need for inner healing.

I explained to him that we perceive separation from natural parents as a total rejection of ourselves. In spite of the love shown by the adoptive or foster parents, there remains an area of emptiness within which nothing seems to touch.

The man remained resistant to this idea, informing me that he had known he was adopted since the age of three; he accepted it and it was no longer a problem. It was with much reluctance, therefore, that he finally agreed to let me pray for this area, resolving to "endure however long it would take" just so he could get out of there.

He later described his experience to me,

> I did not see how the past could have such a tremendous effect on the present or how the unconscious could keep a memory so active and vital even though the conscious had resolved the issue years ago, nor did I see what prayer could do about it anyway.
>
> But something began to happen. . . I began to cry. I was hearing her words from a place deep within me, a place I had never touched before. She spoke to me in the name of my natural mother and father and told me they were sorry for giving me life and then having to give me away, but it was the most loving thing they could do for me. And I forgave them. Then I spoke to my adoptive parents and told them how sorry I was for taking out on them the way I felt toward my natural mother and father, and I opened myself to the love my adoptive parents tried to give me all the years of my life.

This prayer experience brought tremendous release to his spirit. Within a few weeks, he felt layers of darkness being lifted from his inner self as a constant mood of depression was removed and his spiritual life began to take wings. A painful region of his life needed to be set free before he was able to confront the splendor of his hidden self and become the person he was meant to be.

It is important to note that the memories of the past are not erased through this type of prayer. They are transformed by the indwelling presence of Jesus Christ. We can still remember the experiences of pain, sorrow, or separation but they no longer prevent us from getting in touch with the goodness also resident within our being. This awareness of our internal struggles gives us deeper empathy for the problems of others. It is often the case that, as we are being healed of particular memories, the Lord will send others to us who are suffering from similar circumstances in order that we might minister to them.

I recall the early stages of my own spiritual journey when I was seeking inner healing for some of my early childhood memories regarding my mother. Each day I would encounter people asking me to pray for them for healing of a "mother wound." My first instinct was to tell them I was working on a similar prayer project for myself and wouldn't be able to pray effectively for them until I was healed. However, the teachings of Jesus gave me a better perspective. "Give, and there will be gifts for you . . . because the amount you measure out is the amount you will be given back"(Luke 6:38). I came to understand the importance of my willingness to meet the needs of others and, in the process, my own unhealed memories would be touched. As we reach out to alleviate the sufferings of others, we will be given graces to overcome the problems in our own lives.

Praying inner healing prayer for the period of infancy and early childhood has given me much insight into the value of Jesus' gift of his mother, Mary, to all of us.

Jesus understood the importance of a healthy mother/child relationship when he chose to be born of a woman. He could have come to earth as a fully grown man, thus avoiding all the stages of development, but the Bible clearly chronicles the Lord's willingness to conform to the family structure. Jesus lived under the authority of his parents and "increased in wisdom, in stature, and in favor with God and men" (Lk 2:52).

Mary's influence in the life of her son began at the moment she agreed to accept the angel's request and continued to the agony of the cross. Our understanding of a mother's role in the child's emotional growth enables us to recognize Mary's exceptional qualifications for the responsibilities of rearing Jesus. Such a mission would need to be carried out by one who was herself emotionally healthy since, in the Hebrew culture, an infant was exclusively in the mother's care.

Jesus understood from firsthand experience the valuable effects of balanced maternal love and affection. Therefore, one of his final acts before his death on the cross was to present his mother to all of us. When he spoke the words to his beloved disciple, John, "This is your mother" (Jn 19:27), he bequeathed this precious possession to the world. Whenever we would require the warmth and tenderness of a mother's heart, she would be as available to us as she was for her son.

The significance of this action on the part of Jesus became very apparent to me as I became involved in prayer for psychological healing and realized that many wounds from the past stem from disorder in the mother/child relationship which none of the usual methods of counseling seemed to be able to correct.

Time and time again, I have observed dramatic changes in the lives of persons suffering from painful memories regarding their mothers as they asked Jesus to give them his own mother just as he gave her to John. Often they experience a sense of comfort and peace welling from deep within and bringing a feeling of well-being. One person described it as a feeling of finally "belonging" to someone who really cared about her.

I recall praying with a Protestant minister whose work was threatened because of his frequent bouts of depression. He sought professional counseling and became aware that his problem could be traced to the sudden death of his mother when he was three. He was subsequently cared for by a variety of foster parents in home situations where he received very little, if any, demonstrative affection. As he related it, "My childhood seems like a vacuum waiting to be filled with something."

He attended one of our weekend workshops on healing prayer and, on Saturday afternoon, joined the group in the chapel as I prayed a general healing prayer for the various periods of life. He felt no particular response to the prayer until I began to pray for infancy and early childhood. As I asked the Lord to give us his mother to supply anything deficient in our relationship with our own mothers, he became very resistant, believing I was attempting to impose some Catholic devotion on him. At that moment he heard Jesus speaking deep in his heart, "Don't be afraid to accept my mother's love. She won't lead you away from me." A flood of emotions broke over him as he imaged the face of a beautiful woman with tenderness in her eyes, her arms open to receive him. Many years of loneliness were washed away that afternoon as the internal vacuum began to be filled with light.

The woman chosen to bear the son of God was addressed by the angel Gabriel as "highly favored," a distinction which has not faded with the passage of time.

This focus on the role of the mother in early development does not imply that the father's relationship is unimportant. Again we can look to the life of Jesus and the significant contribution of Joseph in caring for his foster son. Joseph stands out as a prime example of the importance of a father's sensitivity to the Holy Spirit. It was his relationship to God as well as his desire to yield himself to the Father's will which brought protection, guidance, and strength into the life of Jesus.

Recent studies are demonstrating the importance of a father's influence regarding the forces which mold a child into a caring adult. Writing in the *New York Times* several years ago, David Coleman reported on findings involving seventy-five men and women who were part of a 1950 study begun by researchers at Yale University in which five-year-olds were tracked into adulthood. Their teachers and mothers were asked to rate their family life, behavior, and personality. Of all the factors studied, the single, most powerful predictor of empathy in adulthood was how much time the children's father spent with them. The report quoted the psychologists as saying, "We were astounded at how strong the father's influence was after twenty-five years. It seems that spending time with the child gives fathers more opportunities to be responsive to the child's needs and so model empathy for them."

All the current studies of parent/child development point to the absence of a father or the inconsistency of his emotional support as a causative factor in juvenile crime in our country.

As previously mentioned, fathers are being given opportunities to share in the birth experience in most hospitals, thus encouraging them to take a more active part in the entire child-rearing process. My husband, Ben, presented a beautiful example of paternal care when our children were babies, never hesitating to hold, play with, feed, and change them whenever the need arose. I attribute much of their emotional stability to the concerted effort we both put forth to give them as much love and attention as was possible.

It seems only reasonable that a child can reach maturity with the least amount of difficulty if he or she has the psychological support of both parents. The infant's loss of either parent, through death or other forms of separation, can cause deep woundedness to the hidden self. But even if we have not experienced such obvious trauma during infancy and early childhood, our unconscious mind may still retain vestiges of unexplained discomfort which present problems for our emotional development. It is much simpler to define the reasons for inner distress when we are aware of situations which brought sadness, sorrow, or separation into our lives.

Persons reared in homes where the parents were basically generous in giving care, who tried as best they could to meet the needs of their offspring, may feel disloyal when they entertain thoughts of parental inadequacies. Yet, as previously mentioned, because of our imperfections, no parent can do a perfect job of caring for a child. Every one of us, regardless of our desire to love our children, has failed at times to meet their needs, leaving them with a vague sense of neglect or lack of love. Infants are essentially self-centered, perceiving everything in their little world as revolving around themselves. Disruptions in this pattern, even though minimal, are usually interpreted as a lack of love, which may subtly distort perceptions long after infancy.

The healing love of Jesus Christ provides us with the answer to this emptiness by supplying our inner being with his perfect love. The following prayer may be a step toward introducing his presence into this portion of our hidden self.

LORD JESUS CHRIST, I ask you to walk
back in time with me to my infancy, bringing the
light of your Holy Spirit into the darkened corners
of my memory. As you illuminate my hidden self,
touch those areas within where I feel a sense of
loneliness and emptiness. The human heart is very
sensitive to the thoughts and feelings of others so I
ask you to heal me of any real or imagined rejection
by my mother, father, or other parental figure
during this stage of development.

If I was separated from either parent because of
illness, death, or other circumstances, release me
from any sense of abandonment and loss. Fill my
inner being with your love.

Jesus, let me know your protective presence
guarding and guiding me during my early life just as
you were given security through the watchful
presence of St. Joseph. Allow me to feel the strong
arms of a father's love surrounding me. If my own
father was unable to demonstrate affection, I ask
you to bring to me the hugging and touching
gestures of a father's hands. You always called the
little children to come sit on your lap; please enable
me to accept this same invitation being spoken to
my inner child.

Lord, I thank you for recognizing my need for the
warmth and tenderness of a mother's love by gifting

me with your own mother, Mary. In those inner regions where I needed more nurturing, place me in the arms of your mother. Ask her to sing me lullabies, to rock me, to tell me little stories, to feed me just as she did for you. Wherever I may have harbored a sense of being neglected, I accept her love to attend to my needs as she gently touches me with a mother's affectionate care.

Jesus, if there were situations of physical or mental abuse in my early years, touch the internal scars of those memories so that through your wounds I might be healed. Grant me the grace to forgive those who did not treat me with kindness and respect just as you forgave those who tormented you.

Lord, if my infancy and early childhood contained episodes of illness and pain, please set me free from the ways in which this marked my life. Surround my sufferings with your comforting presence, assuring me that I am never alone during any trials and turmoil. Increase my faith and trust in your love for me.

I give into your hands this entire portion of my existence, believing that through your infinite mercy it will be brought to wholeness. AMEN.

CHAPTER FIVE

CHILDHOOD

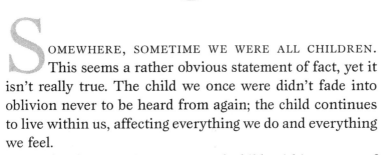

SOMEWHERE, SOMETIME WE WERE ALL CHILDREN. This seems a rather obvious statement of fact, yet it isn't really true. The child we once were didn't fade into oblivion never to be heard from again; the child continues to live within us, affecting everything we do and everything we feel.

Each of us carries an eternal child within, a set of feelings and attitudes brought from childhood that remains operative no matter how old we become. In fact, the more we advance in chronological age, the more we are likely to return to the childish actions which marked our younger days. A few hours spent visiting any local nursing home will confirm that truth.

Our inner child causes us to view life in a somewhat distorted fashion. Our adult, rational mind gives us an intelligent appraisal of a situation, whereas the inner child sees the same circumstances through the emotional context of past experiences. Such divergence can cause much confusion in our decision-making process!

When my husband and I were presented with the opportunity of moving to Florida from our childhood state of Illinois, the adult part of us discussed the possibilities with reason and calm. The decision was made and preparations begun when our inner children began to react with a variety of strong emotions, not the least of which was fear over leaving family and friends for some unfamiliar territory. The shock of these anxieties, coupled with our own children's negative reactions to the move, almost convinced us that we had made a terrible mistake. Nevertheless, we agreed to abide by our original decision, bolstered by the advice and prayers of our more levelheaded friends and relatives. Had our internal fears been permitted to prevail, we would have certainly missed out on a rich opportunity for personal and family growth experiences.

One of the most powerful and pervasive attitudes in our culture regarding childhood is the idea that at some point you cease to be a child and are an adult forever after. This fallacy makes it extremely difficult for many persons to deal with their emotional life. The demand to behave in a grown-up manner implies that we must discard anything which could be construed as immature conduct. Since tears, laughter, and spontaneity are so much a part of our childhood, they must be eradicated from our behavior.

If this is true, why did Jesus teach us, "I tell you most solemnly, unless you change and become like little children you will never enter the kingdom of heaven" (Mt 18:3)? He wasn't asking us to remain in a childish state of development but to allow ourselves to retain the childlike attitudes which make us accessible to the presence of God. The emotions of our inner child, the ability to trust others for our needs, the gifts of wonder and awe are essential to our receptivity of the spiritual world. Much of God's kingdom is unreasonable to our rational, scientific minds, and only the little child within us can venture into this unfamiliar domain.

Yet most adults become very self-critical if they do anything which could be considered childlike. We assume the role of our parents, older relatives, or teachers to mete out punishment to ourselves so it won't happen again. Such punitive measures account for a wide variety of destructive behavior being practiced in the world today.

The "little child" that Jesus is calling forth finds it very difficult to be exposed in our present world structure. Today we don't even permit children to be childlike. In 1963, the Play Schools Association published a booklet which read in part: "Being a child isn't what it once used to be. Huck Finn is a delinquent. Tom Sawyer isn't working up to capacity, and Heidi is in foster care. Jim Hawkins is too young to be a cabin boy, and whoever would let Alice just sit there, doing nothing at all but dream through a summer afternoon? . . . Today's child often walks a tightrope between neglect and pressure. He gets too much stimulation or none at all. He may have forgotten how to play . . . parents worry whether their children will excel before they have left kindergarten." Since that time, pressures on children have only grown.

Never before in history has so much time, attention, money, and energy been spent on the raising of children as in the United States today. Parents spend the majority of their waking hours in chauffeuring, entertaining, and teaching their offspring. At one point in my life, I thought I would have to be surgically removed from behind the wheel of our station wagon because I spent so many hours transporting our five active youngsters from one "meaningful experience" to another.

Yet, in spite of all this attention, most of us would not want to be a child in today's world. Childhood in our society docs not permit the carefree, spontaneous behavior which should characterize this stage of development.

One of the finest books written on this subject is entitled, *The Conspiracy Against Childhood*. It may have been written many years ago (1971), but the message is even more important in today's society. In it Dr. Eda LaShan makes the following observation:

> There is too frequently today a tense and frantic quality in our relationships with our children.

> We often seem to have forgotten how to be, or are afraid of acting like, parents—afraid of guiding and controlling our children's behavior in order for them to become increasingly responsible human beings with a sense of dignity and purpose in life. We do things for them that they should be doing for themselves, such as driving them to school when they ought to walk or apologizing to Grandma about how busy they are when they should have written a thank-you note for the birthday present. On the other hand, we make them do things for which they are totally unready, such as learning numbers and letters at two and a half.

The author poses an interesting theory that, contrary to popular belief, our attitudes of indulgence toward the young do not reflect tenderness and compassion but an extreme desire to eradicate the joys of childhood. The pain within ourselves pertaining to the experiences of our own childhood is being projected upon our offspring. The more we refuse to look at our inner child, denying that he or she even exists, the more we will also attempt to keep the world around us from experiencing true childhood.

Yet, the words of Jesus are quite clear in this regard: it is not possible to become a member of the Father's kingdom without becoming childlike. He tells us we must make ourselves "as little as this little child" (Mt 18:4), implying an act of the will on our part. We have to, in a sense, give ourselves permission to run and laugh and play in our Father's house.

This is an extremely threatening concept for most of us. We've worked so hard to become mature, independent persons and been repeatedly commended for these personality traits. Without the healing love of Jesus Christ, such vulnerability would be impossible for most of us.

Often the memories of childhood erect barriers between us and God's love for us. We are taught by Jesus to address God as our Father but if our concept of father is distorted, we can exert much resistance to this relationship. If our natural father was overly strict, we tend to project this attitude onto our Father in heaven, expecting him to severely discipline us at the slightest provocation. With this type of mentality, we believe God's will for us to be harsh and demanding. Why would we want to yield our lives into the hands of such a deity?

If our natural fathers were unable to demonstrate affection toward us, we perceive ourselves as being unlovable to the rest of the world as well. "The life of a father," says a French writer, "has a mysterious prestige: The hours he spends at home, the room where he works, the objects around him, his pursuits, his hobbies, have a sacred character." We have a tendency to take our mother's presence for granted, probably because we were conditioned to expect her attention, but our father's attitude during childhood can have a strong effect on our self-image. We want to please him, get his attention (especially if there are other brothers and sisters vying for the same privilege). To be the father's favorite child is a goal of every little boy and girl, and we will sometimes go to great lengths to obtain it.

How many women have told me they became proficient in some kind of athletics to attract their father's notice? In a similar vein, I've listened to many men relate their choice of profession to their father's influence.

Literature and drama are filled with stories involving the joy and pain of the father/child relationship (*A Lion in Winter* is an excellent example). The Old Testament provides many opportunities to study the effects of paternal acceptance on the lives of children. Rebekah recognized this truth when she conspired with her son,

Jacob, in obtaining a blessing from his dying father, Isaac. She knew that Jacob could not fulfill his destiny without this important gesture from his father and, even though such favor really belonged to Esau, the mother made sure that Jacob became the chosen one (cf. Gn 27).

Little girls need the affirmation of a father's love if they are to grow up secure in their femininity. Many women are fighting today for something that should rightfully have been given to them many years ago but was withheld for a variety of reasons. True women's liberation has to come from within, the healing of the child who felt rejected and unloved, so women can then work more effectively, with less anger and rebellion, toward a nation which assures the rights of every person.

The large number of persons reporting incestuous relationships came as quite a surprise to me when first I began ministering inner healing prayer. (Incest is formally defined as sexual activity between persons who are related to each other so closely that they are forbidden to marry.) I thought perhaps I was seeing an inordinate number of such cases among the adults I was counseling until discussions with professional counselors in the Association of Christian Therapists convinced me otherwise.

Incest is much more common than we care to admit in our society, and the numbers of reported incidences are certainly escalating. Much of the publicity is due to new freedom in dealing with this situation, but the problem has been around for a long time.

Hank Giarretto, a psychologist in San Jose, California, started a child sexual abuse treatment program for the Santa Clara County juvenile probation department in 1971. At that time, authorities generally estimated the rate of incest to be one case per million population. But out of a county population of slightly more than one million, predominantly middle-class white, with the highest median income of any California metropolitan area, Giarretto in his first year received not one case but thirty. Six years later his case load was above 600. "I believe," he said, "that incest is epidemic in America."

In their book, *Betrayal of Innocence*, Dr. Susan Ford and Craig Bush estimate that their research demonstrates at least ten million people in the United States are victims of incest. Like me, they were initially surprised by the large numbers of clients who were seeking help to overcome these painful wounds of the past. Their years of counseling have convinced them that incest and sexual abuse are deeply repressed in our society.

Because this activity carries such a heavy social stigma, it has been, for many years, the hidden sin in our country. Often the guilt of early sexual encounters weighs so heavily upon people that they refuse even to discuss it during years of therapy with qualified counselors. They are still responding to the commands given to them as children, "If you tell anyone, I'll kill you," or other threats of a similar nature.

A frequent type of incestuous relationship seems to be between girls and older family members—brother, father, grandfather, uncle—but I have also prayed with men who suffered much trauma from sexual activities with the mother or older sister. Homosexual incest among family members is also not uncommon.

In all these situations, deep scars of resentment, confusion, and fear remain operative to cause a lifetime of emotional pain. I know of no cases which require more compassion and long-term supportive and affirming follow-up than persons who have suffered childhood sexual abuse. The fragile ego of the trustful, little child has been severely damaged and only the healing power of Jesus Christ and an environment of love can restore the trust level.

We also cannot ignore the plight of the person who imposes this type of sexual activity on a child. Most often this is not a sin of lust and passion but a reaction to powerlessness in a person's life. As a father remarked on a news report on the subject, "I didn't really want sex. What I wanted was someone who needed me as much as I needed them." If our prayer groups and churches can look beyond the sin to see the brokenness of the sinner, we can help many to discover the cleansing love of Jesus who alone can remove our transgressions from us.

Sometimes the most important gift of healing we can provide for those who have been traumatized by incest is to allow them to finally talk about it. As long as it remains forever the "unforgivable" and "unspeakable" sin, it can never be healed. It is important that we not express righteous indignation or judgment toward the person who is already suffering acute pain. "Fifty per cent of all psychiatry is non-judgmental, loving, listening," according to Morton Kelsey. Listening in this way and inviting Jesus to bring the light of his presence into the darkness of these memories can begin a process which will assure much freedom.

Childhood marks the time when we begin to venture forth into society by attending school. This interaction with persons outside of the immediate family can sometimes create stressful situations which may need to be healed if we are to be comfortable socializing in our adult world. The criticisms and punishments of teachers can cause us to expect the same type of treatment from other authority figures in life—employers, for example, making us continually tense on the job. The competitive grading system which constantly compares us to classmates can produce feelings of inferiority which make it difficult to relate to others on an equal basis.

One prayer group member requested intercessory prayer for her inability to speak up during prayer meetings. She often had a word of scripture or a prophecy for the group but became panic stricken whenever she considered sharing such messages. In discussing the problem, she revealed that it wasn't only a dilemma in the prayer group setting but in every part of her life; she was tongue-tied when more than two persons were in the room.

Further discussion centered on the childhood memories of school experiences where she described much fear and tension associated with one teacher. On one occasion she was not prepared to recite some verses of poetry assigned to be memorized. The teacher then forced her to stand in the aisle with a paper bag on her head for the remainder of the class period. She was terrified at being singled out in this manner, causing her to wet her pants which created much laughter among her classmates. She became the object of many cruel jokes and, as a result of the incident, learned to devise numerous methods to avoid ever having to recite in class again.

It didn't require much detective work to understand the escape mechanism of the child still operating in her adult life and to pray for inner healing of those fearful memories. She gradually began to share her spiritual gifts with the prayer group as the Lord gave her the courage to speak his word.

The relationship with brothers and sisters during childhood can also be a source of conflict for us. The term "sibling rivalry" is a very apt description of the conflict since there is a natural tendency in most of us to compete with other children in our family unit. As previously mentioned, everyone desires to be the favored child. This type of rivalry is not necessarily destructive since the interaction with siblings can be a source of stimulation and challenge. The young brother who tries to imitate the personality of his older and wiser brother has a role model which can be an effective source for growth, especially if the older one is willing to devote some attention to his "little brother."

Nevertheless, there can be elements of pain between siblings which need to be confronted if we are to grow beyond the selfishness of our inner child. The older sister who cared for us when the parents were working may have exerted undue disciplinary measures. The handicapped brother or sister who required much care and attention may have caused us to harbor secret feelings of hatred and resentment toward him or her which need to be brought into the forgiving light of Jesus Christ. Perhaps we require healing concerning a younger brother or sister who always got us into trouble by "tattling" on us so we would be punished instead of them.

Long-term illness or hospitalization is disruptive at any age but especially during the childhood years. Not being able to run and play with the "other kids" can make us feel different, causing feelings of loneliness and isolation. Trying to keep up with class work can present an added strain, which continues to give rise to a sense of inadequacy or incompetency. Being cared for by strangers who were not as gentle or understanding as one's own family can be extremely frightening. All these situations respond very well to the healing touch of Jesus as we invite him to remove the memories of pain, both physical and emotional.

The death of a close family member is also an obviously stressful experience for a person on any level of development. It can remain an unconscious source of inner tension if we were not permitted to grieve by being told to "Act like a man," or "Big girls don't cry." Such injunctions force us to bury many feelings of anger, guilt, and sorrow, making it difficult to deal with our present-day emotions in an honest way.

A participant at one healing seminar requested prayer because of his inability to relate to his two young boys in a fatherly way. He loved them very much but avoided any outward expressions of his feelings for them and he seldom found time to do the kinds of things that fathers and sons should enjoy together. He was really distraught that a Christian parent should be exhibiting such behavior. We talked about his background for a while and he shared that his own father had passed away when he was five years old.

I asked him how he was told that his dad was dead. "My mother told me that Jesus had come to take my daddy to heaven," he replied, "and I would have to be the man of the family now." He never cried at the funeral home or the cemetery as he was told by his grandmother to be a "brave little soldier and make Mommy proud of you." Naturally all those suppressed emotions were still resident in the deep mind. He was unable to relate to his own boys because so much of his inner child had to be denied in order to continue obeying those long-ago commands.

As I prayed with the man, we invited Jesus to give the little boy inside of him permission to mourn for his father and to open up the reservoir of his emotions which had been dammed up for so long. The sobs came from deep within him as he cried out all the loneliness and pain of those growing-up years. It was beautiful to receive a letter from him several months later detailing the adventures he and his sons experienced on a weekend camping trip.

It's interesting to note that death or separation from a loved pet during childhood can also be a source of inner pain. Children do not make the distinctions between animal and human species that adults do. Any living creature can provide a relationship of love which conveys a sense of self-worth and belonging to a child, therefore causing emptiness and pain when it is removed.

One woman I prayed with had endured years of emotional instability which began when her mother punished her for failing to do her household chores by poisoning her pet rabbit. Such cruelty needs to be healed before we can again dare to trust those around us.

The child of divorced parents generally faces deep feelings of insecurity, anger, and loneliness. Trying to keep his or her balance in the midst of the surrounding turmoil often creates a stress reaction which is sometimes acted out by misbehaving in school, stealing, or lying—deliberate efforts to gain some attention to relieve the inner pain. Children feel an acute sense of responsibility for the happiness of their parents since so much of their security resides within the cohesiveness of the family unit. Therefore, if the relationship between parents breaks down, the child feels guilty that his or her love was not sufficient to heal the breach between mother and father. The burden of this false guilt needs to be released or it will often continue to elicit feelings of condemnation and failure beyond the childhood stage.

Insecurity may also surface if the family moved frequently, making it difficult to develop friendships and sink roots. Granger Westberg, in his very helpful little book on the grieving process, *Good Grief*, states, "We who have spent years teaching in hospital and medical centers see a great many sick or upset people who have come into the hospital in close relation to such an uprooting experience (as moving from one area to another). I have seen children who are thrown into turmoil three months before the move and for three months or more after the move." In asking the Lord to heal us of childhood distress, this area should not be overlooked.

Each of us can add to this list his or her own particular feelings from childhood memories. Some of these remembrances are easy to recall and we can specifically bring them into the healing love of Jesus Christ. Others have become cloudy and indistinguishable in the recesses of our deep mind. Regardless of what lies buried within us, the Holy Spirit is able to unravel fact from fantasy and lead us into all truth.

LORD JESUS CHRIST, I ask you to go back with me in my life to the period of time known as childhood. It was you who directed me to make myself as a little child; therefore, help me to overcome any resistance in me against becoming childlike again.

Touch all the ways I was ordered to "act grown-up," commands which gave me the impression that everything in childhood was unacceptable behavior. Help me to recapture the wonder and awe of the little child within me. Allow me to again delight in the beauty of the world you created as I draw comfort from gazing at clouds, butterflies, and flowers. Let my spirit rejoice in the song of the birds and the warm, summer breezes as all of creation whispers your name.

Lord, heal me of any difficulties I may have toward addressing God as Father. If a relationship with my natural father brought fear, let your perfect love for me cast out the tension and anxiety of the past so I can approach the Father with trust and openness of heart. If my natural father was distant, rejecting, or unaffirming, please fill those empty areas within me with your positive, affirming presence. Speak to me as you did through the prophet Isaiah, "I have called you by your name and you are mine. . . . Because you are precious in my eyes, because you are honored and I love you" (Is 43:2-3). Enable me to believe this truth about myself, that I am very dear to you.

Jesus, you were indignant when the disciples tried to stop little children from climbing into your lap. "Let the little children alone, and do not stop them coming to me; for it is to such as these that the kingdom of heaven belongs" (Mt 19:14). You were never too busy to touch a child, to play, to tell stories; please touch me in that way today. Let the little child within me respond to your invitation to "come to you" abandoning all my resistance to your love. Let me trust in the friendship we share with one another as you heal me of the childhood memories of relationships which wounded and frightened me.

Please bless all the members of my family today and every day as you help me to see them through your eyes. If I harbor resentments against brothers or sisters, give me your forgiving love to set me free from those obstacles to grace. Any feelings toward my parents which are not touched with peace I pray you to bring into your light and love. Whether my parents are still on this earth or have gone to be with you, let them know that the relationship between us is surrounded with your reconciling Spirit.

If I was wounded by classroom experiences which continue to affect my interaction with others, bring the light of your love into those situations. Allow me to feel your presence with me during the school years, as I image you sitting with me at my desk, assisting me with my studies and protecting me against any threats from classmates or teachers.

Release me from the pain of any physical or sexual
abuse brought upon me by others. Jesus, you know
the shame and embarrassment that still burns
within me because of this violation against me.
Help me to feel your gentle touch absolving me
from any sense of "sin," washing me clean,
restoring my self-worth once again. As in the psalm,

> Purify me with hyssop until I am clean;
>
> wash me until I am whiter than snow.
>
> Instill some joy and gladness into me,
>
> let the bones you have crushed rejoice again.
>
> Hide your face from my sins,
>
> wipe out all my guilt
>
> and create a clean heart in me.
>
> —Psalms 51:7–10

Help me to believe that I am cleansed of all
defilement through your precious blood. Give me
the grace to overcome feelings of resentment and
betrayal so I can begin to trust others again.

Jesus, if my spirit is still grieving for a loved one
who died when I was a child, please relieve me of
this burden. Enable me to finally release this person
into your arms, believing that one day we will meet
again in heaven. Comfort me with your love so all
the sadness and sorrow can truly be turned into joy.

Let all that is associated with my childhood be
brought into union with you so all that is good
may remain and all that creates barriers
might be removed.

I believe that you will continue to bless this area of
my life with all the grace necessary for healing,
bringing about these answers to my prayer in your
way and in your time. AMEN.

CHAPTER SIX

ADOLESCENCE

ADOLESCENCE IS THAT PERIOD FROM AGE TWELVE to twenty when a person grows from childhood to adulthood.

It sounds so simple when presented in those terms but it is, in reality, an excruciatingly painful time of development for most persons. The inner tensions and outer stresses experienced during this period are generally more demanding than any other we encounter during our entire life. Recent statistics bear witness to this fact with the alarming report that suicide is now the second cause of death among the fifteen to twenty-five age group in the United States. Being young does not mean being problem free!

Since our five children were born within a six year span, we were blessed with having all of them pass through the teen years together. Any rose-colored illusions I may have carried over from my own high school years were quickly shattered as we faced the daily crises of their conflicts. I well remember our middle daughter, Beth, at age fifteen sitting on her bed and pouring out her heart as she cried, "I don't understand what's happening to me! I've got all kinds of feelings I never had before!"

That statement defines the sum and substance of the adolescent process, trying to sort out overwhelming feelings in an effort to bring them into some kind of manageable control. It can be a most frightening task if not undergirded with much emotional support from parents, teachers, and other trusted adults.

Sixteen-year-olds often go through the equivalent of a nervous breakdown as they attempt to cope with the myriad impulses reacting continually with their nervous systems. In the midst of trying to deal with their accelerated physical growth (if only clothes were designed to expand during adolescence!), they are faced with the need to contend with a variety of emotions which are new to them. All this is complicated by the pressure to excel in class work, make the basketball team, get a part-time job, and decide on a career choice. While they are struggling through all this confusion, Aunt Suzy comes for a visit and remarks, "Enjoy yourself, honey, these are the best years of your life." No wonder they think grownups are dumb. No wonder they shrink at the prospect of entering adulthood if this is the best life has to offer.

Although the pressures exerted upon today's young people are certainly more evident than in previous generations, our own journey through adolescence was no less painful in many respects. The desire for independence from parental influences and the need to make decisions freely have always created tensions between parents and offspring. Sometimes we fail to recognize the powerful effects our adolescent behaviors continue to exert on our adult lives.

Sally (not her real name) was a member of our prayer community. She was a vibrant, outgoing young woman who seemed to have everything going for her. Yet, she found a way to sabotage every job opportunity and close relationship. In spite of a college degree, she was working as a cashier in a movie theatre. She dated many young men but always broke off the friendship before it could become too much of a commitment. In desperation, one afternoon she came to my house for prayer. She told me about her teenage years when she ran away from home at sixteen and lived on the street. She had been determined to prove to her parents that she could take care of herself.

Eventually Sally returned home and completed her education but the scars of her experiences caused her to erect emotional barriers around herself. "I hate the things I did and I hate myself for being such a fool." We had several prayer sessions asking Jesus to release her from the bondage of teenage foolishness. Within a year she began to break out of her self-imposed prison and find a more suitable means of employment. Eventually she ran for public office (which she won), served on the city council for many years, and married an affluent businessman.

Deciding to "do my own thing" and "find myself" are about as new as the Prodigal Son and they continue to produce much the same results. Wildly abandoning ourselves to internal impulses will never satisfy the true hunger which is longing for spiritual liberation. St. Augustine lived on the level of self-gratification for more than forty years before he finally realized, "Our hearts will never be at rest until they rest in thee, O Lord." The story of his constant battle against the world, the flesh, and the devil should be a source of comfort to all parents who see their children moving in directions away from the Lord.

This man, who became a doctor of the church, always attributed his conversion to the faithful prayers of his mother, Monica. We can never underestimate the importance of parents' prayers in keeping the protective love of Jesus surrounding their children. It's my belief that when the Lord sends us children, he also gives us spiritual authority over their lives so our prayers for them contain special power over the wiles of the evil one. It's a fortunate child whose parents understand this truth.

The conflict of wills between parents and children often creates a power struggle which can lead to many altercations. In a home where the parents understand that they are being tested by their offspring, they will maintain their position in spite of argument and give stability to their youngsters' lives. Most often adolescents are crying out for help since they themselves cannot control their emotions, and they desperately need to know that someone will do it for them. Children really believe a parent cares when healthy discipline is employed even if they outwardly continue to act rebellious.

Babe Ruth, who was educated at St. Mary's Industrial School in Baltimore, once commented, "The more I think of it, the more important I feel it is to give kids 'the works' as far as religion is concerned. They may never be holy, they may act like tough monkeys, but somewhere inside will be a solid little chapel. It may get dirty from neglect, but the time will come when the door will be opened with much relief. But the kids can't take it if we don't give it to them."

How often I've heard friends of our children remark that "So-and-So's parents don't *care* about him because he can do anything he wants." At home they probably tell their parents that this person is really lucky to have so much freedom as they plead for fewer restraints. Such is the apparent ambivalence of this stage.

The clash of parent/child wills can have a carry-over effect into adulthood if it becomes a destructive form of behavior. Many persons have spent the majority of adult life trying to prove to one or the other parent that they were "independent." While this attitude is important in the initial stages of detachment, and honest respect for our parents should always remain active within us, there comes a point where seeking to please the Lord should be our primary motivator. The inner struggle to let this happen in us can sometimes show us areas where conflicts between parent and child were never resolved in a healthy way, and we are unconsciously still attempting to assert ourselves over their authority. If arguments were not eventually concluded with an expression of reconciliation, such as a warm hug, even though the differences of opinion may remain, the breach between parent and child can cause inner anguish making it difficult to move on to the next level of development. Unconsciously we still strive in various ways to bring about closure for these wounded feelings, a state which can induce a lot of mental energy to be drained from us. Arguments in the teenage years are inevitable but, handled with equal measures of firmness and love, they can enable us to learn useful ways of dealing with our anger.

The problems encountered in living in a household where no angry feelings were permitted to surface and everyone denied these emotions with a variety of "games" can also bring crippling behavior in later life. A person with this type of background who marries one who was raised to openly express feelings at every opportunity may become very intimidated and withdrawn. Much of the counseling in today's mental health clinics centers around the importance of feelings as they relate to maturity.

I worked for a year in a psychiatric hospital where we spent hours helping patients to relieve their symptoms of distress by showing them the causes of their behavior. The work was very frustrating because understanding the root of their problems brought so little relief to many of them. After I became involved in healing prayer and learned about inner healing, it was clear to me that this was the missing element. To understand why I do something may only be the first step; true liberation comes when I can invite Jesus to set me free from the bondages of the past. God gave us very rich emotions but they can become truly creative as we allow him to teach us how to bring them into balance.

I recall praying with a middle-aged businessman who was complaining of anxiety episodes affecting his work. There were the usual pressures from his daily routine but nothing which could account for the waves of fear increasingly attacking him.

As we discussed his life, he described himself as very bullheaded and strong-willed, stating that this sometimes got him into trouble. I asked for an example and he related a long-remembered teenage argument between him and his father over the use of the family car. In spite of his father's warnings, he drove the car anyway, was involved in an accident and "totaled" it. Fortunately, he was not injured but arrived back home to see an ambulance pulling out of his driveway with lights flashing and sirens sounding. His father died of a heart attack on the way to the hospital and there was never an opportunity for them to reconcile their differences.

I explained that it was important to bring closure to that experience and perhaps this would have some effect on his anxiety episodes. "How can I make peace with my father when he's dead?" he asked. Very simply I told him that the Lord Jesus Christ, who is the only mediator between God and mankind (1 Tm 2:5), could be his reconciler. "Ask Jesus to tell your father how sorry you are for disobeying him," I said, "and ask the Lord to forgive you for the disobedience against your dad." The prayer was very brief with very little expression of emotion, but I have learned that the healing power of Jesus Christ is not dependent upon the feelings experienced at the time of prayer. Often there is a time-lapse before the unconscious mind becomes touched and set free. Agnes Sanford, the spiritual writer who has done so much to teach about inner healing, has named the unconscious mind, "Junior." Agnes says, "Sometimes it takes a while before Junior gets the healing message but we must trust the Lord that nothing can hinder the prayer of faith."

In the case of the businessman, several days later he phoned to describe a dream of the previous night in which Jesus was standing with his arm around the man's father. Both were smiling and the Lord said, "Don't worry, Barry, it's all right now." He awoke with the most beautiful sense of peace which seemed to indicate some type of release. At last report, the anxiety attacks had been occurring with less frequency and he was continuing to seek the Lord's will for his life.

This example brings to light the need for forgiveness in the process of healing the hidden self. There is *nothing* that will impede our ability to pray for ourselves or for others more than the unwillingness to forgive. It acts as an invisible barrier between us and the Father which prohibits his blessings from being showered upon us or the ones for whom we pray. It's interesting to note that society has discovered the importance of forgiveness. I was astonished at the number of Web sites dedicated to assisting people with the forgiveness process. There is even a International Forgiveness Institute established in 1994 as an outgrowth of the social science research done at the University of Wisconsin by Robert Enright and his colleagues. They work in such varied domains as the peace movement, the legal profession, English literature, psychotherapy, education, and other disciplines.

If anyone had a "right" to bitterness and hurt feelings it was Jesus. He was mocked, tortured, and scorned by the multitudes, deserted by most of his friends and relatives, yet, in his final moments of extreme physical agony, he prayed, "Father, forgive them; they do not know what they are doing" (Lk 23:34). Jesus knew that his redemptive act would not be complete unless his human nature forgave everyone who had anything to do with his crucifixion.

In the same way, offering our lives to the Father and asking him to heal our hidden self can be impeded when we refuse to forgive. It is a normal phase of adolescence to blame our parents (and other authority figures) for all our misery. We feel victimized and powerless; therefore, it becomes imperative to focus on something outside of ourselves as the perpetrator of our pain. Parents become the natural target as we hold them accountable for our unhappiness.

If this attitude continues into adulthood, becoming habitual, it prevents maturity on the emotional level. Blaming others for our actions, refusing to accept responsibility for our behavior, implies that we remain stranded in the adolescent stage. Forgiving those whom we perceived to be the cause of our problems can be a big step in learning how to deal more effectively with our emotional lives.

It can also enable us to keep the commandment of honoring (respecting) our parents. Interestingly, this is the only commandment which contains a promise, "Honor your father and mother, as Yahweh your God has commanded you, so that you may have long life and may prosper in the land that Yahweh your God gives to you" (Dt 5:16). We actually do ourselves a disservice when we fail to heed this injunction since we deny the blessings pledged to us by God.

Peer pressure, the need to be accepted by classmates and friends, is a predominant characteristic of young people. Feelings of self-consciousness are so pervasive that we don't want to do *anything* which might call attention to ourselves (outside of athletic contests where individuality is tolerated). Conforming to the group connotes our acceptance as a worthwhile person and we try very hard to maintain that position throughout adolescence. I can still recall the baby-blue vinyl jackets and white buck shoes that we wore to high school. What a status symbol that was!

While these juvenile identification methods are basically harmless, what about the person who never feels accepted by his or her peers? What happens to the one who travels through adolescence as a loner, perhaps leaving school before graduation? Such situations often lead to a sense of worthlessness and inferiority which persists throughout later life.

The cruelty of fellow classmates in the remarks they make to one another, and the jokes played on one another, cut deeply into the fragile ego of an adolescent leaving wounds not easily healed. Being laughed at in the locker room for an underendowed body (this pertains to both sexes) can convince a young person that he or she really doesn't "measure up," thus prohibiting healthy sexual adjustment.

The poignant stories of young romance might make interesting novels but, in reality, they often contain much pain. I recall praying with a young man who was having many problems relating to his wife. He absolutely could not believe she loved him, and no matter how hard she tried, a part of him remained suspicious and unconvinced. The situation was resolved when we asked Jesus to heal him of the feelings of rejection he experienced when a high school sweetheart jilted him for another guy. The memories of that episode had caused him so much pain he determined never to trust a girl again. Such a decision is taken quite seriously by the deep mind which then sends out signals of warning each time the possibility of a trust relationship looms on the horizon. The period of adolescence often contains many memories of broken relationships, broken promises, and broken hearts. Bringing such memories into the light of God's love and allowing him to heal the hurt can relieve us of much pain.

What about the person who entered into destructive behavior, such as drinking, drugs, stealing, or sexual promiscuity, in order to prove his or her independence? The guilt which results from these conditions needs to be resolved or the self-image will continue to suffer. Confessing our wrongdoing, particularly in the sacrament of reconciliation (as discussed earlier in this book), can bring abundant blessings. The Lord is longing to release us of the chains from the past, but he will not usurp our free will in order to give us anything. Looking over the Holy City, he cried, "Jerusalem, Jerusalem . . . How often have I longed to gather your children, as a hen gathers her chicks under her wings, and you refused!" (Mt 23:37). There is an act of our will involved in permitting Jesus to absolve us of our rebellious nature in order to give us new life. He patiently waits for us to cease trying to perfect ourselves, finally yielding our hidden nature into his hands so he can bring us peace.

The rapid sexual development which occurs during adolescence can be a great source of conflict. How to handle these powerful emotions is a subject frequently discussed by teens themselves. False information and experimentation can bring much suffering in later life.

Many persons are unable to form or maintain a healthy and loving sexual relationship due to the distorted sexual attitudes handed down to them by their parents. These attitudes can swing from strict prohibition to open encouragement and permissiveness, either pole reflecting a confused view of sexuality.

I obviously cannot examine all the many ways in which our early training affects adult sexuality. The shelves of today's bookstores are crammed with material on the subject as we rush to compensate for years of cultural taboo with an explosion of literature. For our purposes, as it pertains to inner healing prayer, problems with sexuality *can* be healed and brought into balance by the Lord.

This becomes apparent when we consider that Jesus was resurrected from the dead with all the elements of his humanity intact; his sexuality is part of his resurrected presence. We can ask him to infuse that part of our nature with his completeness, to heal us of negative influences, false attitudes, and fear-filled injunctions.

Again, the importance of Mary, the mother of Jesus, becomes obvious to those of us who represent the female sex. It is a little difficult to identify with the male sexuality of Jesus, but we can ask him to bless our femininity in the same way he touched Mary's when he overshadowed her with the Holy Spirit as she agreed to become the mother of the Savior. Her womanhood was perfected by the Father because she was not afraid to yield that portion of her being into his care.

The many passages of scripture which liken our spiritual lives to the marriage relationship can be valuable sources of meditation for the process of healing the hidden self. One which I have found to be particularly good for women experiencing a poor self-concept is from Isaiah.

> You are to be a crown of splendor in the hand of
> Yahweh,
> a princely diadem in the hand of your God;
> no longer are you to be named "Forsaken,"
> nor your land "Abandoned,"
> but you shall be called "My Delight"

and your land "The Wedded";

for Yahweh takes delight in you

and your land shall have its wedding.

Like a young man marrying a virgin,

so will the one who built you wed you,

and as the bridegroom rejoices in his bride,

so will your God rejoice in you.

—Isaiah 62:3-5

Jesus wants to heal us in order to allow our sexuality to be a source of life, not a barrier to life. Learning to accept our manhood and womanhood in the fullness of its sexual nature, even for those who are unmarried, can produce wellsprings of creativity. Much of my work is with persons who have accepted the celibate life of sister, priest, or brother. Their vocation is never really complete until they confront their sexuality, embrace it, and learn to integrate it into their commitment to the Lord.

The adolescent world is unpredictable, confusing, and frightening, filled with continual tensions, but it also provides challenges which bring us to a deeper understanding of ourselves, God, and others. Life holds no guarantees against pain; I have a motto in my office which says "No pain, no gain." The sufferings we encounter help us to become more sensitive to the world around us as well as to the spiritual world. Being protected from every form of psychological trauma will not cause us to be better integrated human beings, just as isolating an infant in a totally germfree environment won't prepare it for physical life on this planet. As our bodies learn to adjust to microorganisms, we acquire immunity against many illnesses; as our minds learn to confront the constant problems of daily life, we acquire wisdom and understanding. Running away from the natural consequences of life upon this earth through drugs, alcohol, or other escape mechanisms may prolong the process of adolescence far beyond the ordinary time, keeping us perpetually insecure and frightened.

Let us allow the Lord to heal the ways in which we are still hung-up by adolescent experiences creating barriers in the hidden self.

LORD JESUS CHRIST, I ask you to go back in my life to that period between childhood and adulthood known as adolescence and begin to heal me of any hurtful memories from that time. Let the light of your Spirit shine into the shadowy recesses of my deep mind to reveal any area that yet needs to be cleansed and set free.

If there were moments of behavior which still create feelings of shame and embarrassment for me, I ask you, Jesus, to wash away my guilt through your precious blood which was poured out for the forgiveness of my sins. If it would be helpful for me to receive sacramental absolution, please give me the strength to confess my transgressions. In whatever ways my inner being has felt unclean, I thank you for your purifying love which washes me whiter than snow.

Jesus, I ask you to release me from feelings of rejection experienced during this period of my life. The times I felt excluded from "the group," teased or laughed at, made to feel different. Help me to believe that I really do "belong" to a heavenly kingdom where there is no distinction between persons, where all are acceptable. Give me the image of myself that you have; through you I am made worthy of eternal life, therefore, I am a worthwhile member of God's community. Teach me not to ask "Who am I?" but "Whose am I?" as you show me to whom I really belong.

Jesus, there was often much tension between me and my parents during adolescence. Our wills clashed as I attempted to become independent of their values and live my own life. While I understand this is a normal characteristic of the teenage years, I ask you to touch the unhealed memories of arguments and misunderstandings which caused pain between us and were never adequately resolved. Perhaps I still harbor resentment against them for their harsh discipline or unkind remarks. If reconciliation needs to be expressed in the form of a letter, phone call, or visit, give me the courage to take the steps which will bring peace.

Help me to stop blaming others for my failures in life and begin to assume responsibility for my own behavior. Bring my rebellious teenager to the foot of your cross willing to be yielded into your care, no longer saying, "I'd rather do it myself."

Jesus, I thank you for the love you show to me as you bring this area of my life into the warmth of your presence. I trust you to continue this process of healing as I remain close to you in every way possible. AMEN.

CHAPTER SEVEN

EARLY ADULTHOOD

WE'VE ARRIVED AT LAST, ALL GROWN UP AND ready for life! (As if we haven't been living during previous stages of development.) In spite of protestations to the contrary, we have not really completed our growth, nor will we ever do so. The often quoted, "Please be patient, God isn't finished with me yet!" could apply to the adult stage of life as well as to the others.

This stage is the longest in our life span. According to current actuarial tables, a twenty-five-year-old can anticipate at least fifty more years of life on earth. This time is not a period of psychological passivity but one presenting rich opportunities for emotional and spiritual development for those who choose continued growth.

Many aspects of adulthood increase our awareness of the world around us. As we become detached from family ties, join the work force, and begin to establish committed relationships, we are compelled to make choices and face issues and responsibilities which are new to us. Meeting the daily demands of adult living, learning how to confront problems in relationships, and accepting responsibility for our behavior, can all be means to deeper psycho-spiritual development. Adulthood presents us with ample opportunities to imitate Jesus who "increased in wisdom, in stature and in favor with God and men" (Lk 2:52) as he permitted himself to enter the maturation process.

The struggles we face during this period of life can be an important step in drawing us closer to God and to one another. If life contained no difficulties, we could remain self-sufficient and locked into our own little worlds, never venturing out to discover the hidden areas of strength within our nature. But we are called into the light of self-awareness when we become willing to face inner pain and outer sorrow in order to continue to grow. Unfortunately, today's society does not always understand the value of confronting reality. It is common to drop out through drugs, alcohol, and illicit sexual encounters. These solutions don't really confer peace, joy, patience, and love to our world but only mask the symptoms of disorder and delay the healing we all need.

It is nearly impossible to obtain emotional and spiritual maturity without some kind of pain associated with it. Yet we have been saturated with the myth of material happiness, making us confused and frustrated when troubles come our way. So many childhood fairy tales end with "and they lived happily ever after," that we approach adulthood expecting only joy. If the marriage relationship shows areas of disagreement or the job selection isn't what we expected, the common response is to dump the present situation and seek the replacement which will make us happy. Because we so completely accept the happiness myth, we assume everyone around us has found contentment, that all our friends, neighbors, and coworkers really have it all together.

No one has it all together; not the businessman, the spiritual leader, or the career woman. All face the same needs and desires for fulfillment. We often become convinced, however, that our encounters with problems in adulthood must indicate instability because we fail to recognize the normality of adjustment periods in everyone's life. This response causes us to become fearful of exposure, believing there must be something terribly wrong with us. We learn to wear the mask of self-sufficiency and become more and more isolated from the kinds of situations which could enable us to grow.

The thought of allowing others to learn of our inner confusions and doubts fills us with such terror that we avoid confrontation through a variety of psychological mechanisms. Mary Tyler Moore's portrayal of the mother in the film *Ordinary People* is an excellent example of one kind of denial response. Rather than face herself, she chose to escape through separating from the husband and son who were calling her to honest confrontation. The fault with such actions lies in the fact that it is impossible to leave our problems with self behind; we may change the scenery but the inner character remains the same.

Learning the value of sharing our hidden self with others can be of much assistance in continuing growth during adulthood. Having at least one other person, be it spouse or friend, who can share the intimate areas of our thoughts and feelings, can do much to lend strength and support to the times of doubt and uncertainty. Women are generally much better at forming these types of friendships than men.

I live in an area of Florida where there are many retirees. It isn't unusual to observe men sitting silently, side by side on the benches at the mall, for hours at a time, as they wait for their wives to finish shopping. When a conversation does develop, it generally has to do with sports or the weather. These are apparently considered "safe subjects."

Previous generations had family units, grandparents, aunts, uncles, and cousins all living in the same area and lending mutual support to one another. Today's society provides little opportunity for the development of such structures as families have become far more mobile. The need to participate in some kind of unified community is cited by young people as the primary reason for their involvement in gang activity. Certainly this need persists in the hearts of all persons, presenting a real challenge to today's religious and secular society.

Learning how to share life with others can even affect our physical life, as Dr. James Lynch, professor of psychology at the University of Maryland, explains in his book, *A Cry Unheard: New Insights into the Medical Consequences of Loneliness.* Using modern technology to study coronary care patients, he was surprised to discover that the simple act of touching a patient to record his pulse rate had the power to completely suppress arrhythmias (abnormal heart rhythms). Dr. Lynch continued his research in numerous coronary care units, compiling copious data which convinced him of the value of human companionship in keeping persons well. He states, "Chronic loneliness and social isolation as well as the loss of a loved one is one of the leading causes of premature death in our country, particularly in the case of heart disease, the nation's number one killer . . . every year millions die, quite literally, of a broken or lonely heart."

Human relationships do seem to matter much more than we realize. The news media are constantly reminding us of our need to diet, exercise, quit smoking, and get regular medical checkups, but seldom are we told that the failure to establish meaningful relationships in our adult life can be hazardous to our health. The opposite appears to be true—there seems to be a concerted effort to convince us of the need to "do your own thing" by not concerning yourself with others except when absolutely necessary.

Often we shun relationships with others because we have been deeply wounded by the failure of a marriage or the loss of a spouse through death. Even the dissolution of a close friendship can cause us to shut the door on intimacy, keeping others at a safe distance from our hidden self. We resolve never to allow anyone to get that close to us again, erecting all manner of barriers to love and life.

This creates difficulties in our earthly relationships but also in the heavenly ones, for "a man who does not love the brother that he can see cannot love God whom he has never seen" (1 Jn 4:20). Opening our hearts to God is very hard to do when we are unable or unwilling to open our hearts to other human beings. Sometimes we need the healing touch of Jesus to relieve us of the pain suffered in broken relationships before we can dare become vulnerable again. Often we need the forgiving love of God to forgive those who have caused us to be wounded in our attempts to relate to others.

Adult life may contain many occasions which produce loneliness, frustration, and pain because we feel no one understands what we are experiencing. We can allow these situations to cause us to become recluses, angry at God and the world for our condition, or we can choose to discover the gift of a new life as we turn these areas over to the Lord, asking him to bring good out of our pain.

Jesus repeatedly asked his followers to "have faith in God," exhorting them to believe that their heavenly Father would assist them in their trials. Since the word "faith" literally means to trust, it implies an attitude of openness and yielding to his presence as we submit our humanity, with its frailties, into his care.

Trust sometimes ceases to operate because we have been disillusioned by the outcome of some of our early adult choices for marriage or profession. We set goals which were not achieved, we had dreams which were not realized, and our hidden self is frustrated and depressed.

I recall praying with one woman who was having a particularly difficult time recuperating from the effects of her divorce. Current research indicates that the stress factor in divorce is higher than that encountered in the loss of a spouse. Both situations involve grieving, but divorce is complicated by an overwhelming sense of failure which plays havoc with the self-image. In this woman's story, her

marriage was dissolved and annulled by the church because
of her husband's infidelity. Yet she was unable to get out
from under a constant feeling of guilt about it all. She
continually accused herself of causing the breakup and
required many months of empathetic care by relatives and
friends before she could begin to forgive herself and feel
loved once more.

In my book, *Healing the Wounds of Divorce,* I detail the
various emotions experienced when a relationship ends.
Not only is the stress factor higher, it's been shown that the
grief level of a divorced person is greater than that of
someone who loses a spouse through death. Even people
who have never faced the trauma of divorce have had some
type of broken relationship in life. I've frequently prayed
with individuals who still carry the wound of an
unfulfilled teenage romance long afterward.

The sorrow of rejection and loss is very deep. It's
interesting to note that when Jesus was dying on the cross,
he didn't cry out about his physical pain but agonizingly
questioned the Father, "My God, my God, why have you
deserted me?" The pain of separation is immeasurable.

The loving support of others who can allow a grieving
person to express feelings of pain and loneliness will
greatly assist the healing process. Sometimes we become
impatient with ourselves and others when little progress
appears evident in our ability to overcome a burden of
grief, failing to recognize the many factors involved in the
process. Jesus promised to "comfort those who mourn," but
it requires time for the aches of the heart to find peace.

I have sometimes prayed with persons experiencing a
sense of grief due to the loss of employment, for this
situation also conveys a feeling of emptiness and
worthlessness. One man was completely incapable of
seeking out another job because of his extreme depression
over being fired. Only the grace of the Lord was sufficient

to bring him the courage needed to overcome his fears and try again. He subsequently discovered a position much more suitable to his talents than the previous one had been.

The feelings of loss associated with the detachment of children is another area of concern for many persons. Much of parental life revolves around the constant care of children. The removal of this responsibility, even though it may bring relief from pressure, still creates a void. Parents often sense that they have lost meaning for their lives, that they are no longer useful or necessary to the human race.

All of my five children are grown, married, and have families of their own. Yet I can still recall the sense of emptiness as each one left the nest and became an independent adult. On the wall of my living room hangs a plaque which has brought much comfort to my heart. It says, "There are two lasting bequests we can give our children, one is roots and the other wings." The roots are easy, it's the wings that present the challenge.

All of us have been subject to disappointments when a dream fails to materialize or a goal is not achieved. We can allow this to cause us to abandon all efforts for personal, family, and communal growth, or we can look to the Lord for a new strength and courage to persevere. The concerns and crises of adult life can teach us to live with the imperfections of ourselves and others, learning not to place unrealistic expectations on spouses, children, and friends. Love always carries the risk of pain since no one, except the Lord, is capable of loving us perfectly.

Recently I ran across a quote attributed to TV interviewer Phil Donahue, "There are really three stages to commitment. There's the fun stage, where you go out and say 'I love doing this.' Then there's stage two, where you become totally intolerant of everybody who doesn't agree with you. Then there's the third stage: the sudden realization that you are not going to make much of a dent.

That's the phase where the saints are made; people who hang in at that point, instead of peeling off and living under a cartop in New Mexico—people who struggle."

We need to ask Jesus to grant us the gift of hope in a fresh outpouring of grace to meet the challenges of hopelessness and despair that sometimes paralyze our lives. It is often much easier to succumb to the darkness of tunnel vision than to permit the Lord to expand our world view as we discipline ourselves to tune into his plan for our lives.

An old story illustrating my point tells of four candles who could be heard speaking to one another. The first candle says, "I am Peace, but these days nobody wants to keep me lit." Then peace's flame slowly diminishes and goes out completely. The second candle says, "I am Faith, but these days I am no longer indispensable." Then Faith's flame slowly diminishes and goes out completely. Sadly, the third candle speaks, "I am Love and I haven't the strength to stay lit any longer. People put me aside and don't understand my importance. They even forget to love those who are nearest to them." And waiting no longer, the Love candle went out completely.

Suddenly, a child enters the room and sees the three candles no longer burning. The child begins to cry, "Why are you not burning? You are supposed to stay lit until the end of time." Then the fourth candle speaks gently to the little child. "Don't be afraid, for I am Hope, and while I still burn, we can relight the other candles." With shining eyes the child took the candle of hope and lit the other three candles.

Only as we permit the Holy Spirit to bring us hope and inspire us with continued courage can we dare to face the pressures of today's world. Spending daily quiet time and listening to God's "still, small voice" can allow us to see the world through his eyes and not with our own limited vision. "Now we are seeing a dim reflection in a mirror, but then we shall be seeing face to face. The knowledge that I have now is imperfect, but then I shall know" (1 Cor 13:12).

Walking in the light of the presence of Jesus Christ as he takes us through the stages of life can help to remove the barriers which keep us from attaining the renewed life promised us in the word of God. Jesus never misled us by indicating that the way would be easy; he told us to expect to carry our cross just as he did. However, he did promise to be with us to lend love and support whenever we asked for his assistance. The responsibility for "seeking, knocking, and finding" rests on our shoulders; the answers rest with him.

LORD JESUS CHRIST, I ask you to bless those areas of my adult life which need to be transformed so that I may reflect your presence in everything I do. Give me the gift of faith to believe that you are aware of every facet of my existence. Help me to know that I can trust you with my life since you will "not break the crushed reed, nor put out the smoldering wick" (Is 42:3).

Lord, there have been moments of pain in my adult life which sometimes made it hard for me to be open to you and to others. The broken promises of a marriage relationship may have left me bitter and hurt; the death of a loved one may have brought sorrow; the breaking up of a friendship may have caused loneliness; the detachment of children may have brought emptiness.

Jesus, please touch my broken heart with the love from your Sacred Heart; give me, in a mystical sense, a real heart transplant. You promised if I would come to you with my heavy burdens, you would give me rest, for your "yoke is easy and your burden light" (Mt 11:30). I admit to being overburdened with the responsibilities and pressures of my daily life; please grant me the ability to place all that I am and all that I ever hope to be into your compassionate care.

Jesus, suffering has often permitted cynicism and doubt to creep into my mind. I have felt hopeless and oppressed, unable to see the world through your eyes. Help me to believe the truth written in your word, "For now I create a new heavens and a new earth, and the past will not be remembered and will come no more to men's minds. Be glad and rejoice for ever and ever for what I am creating" (Is 65:17–18).

Lord, grant me a fresh infusion of hope, to believe, even when I do not see the evidence, that you are bringing goodness into my life.

Jesus, many of my dreams and aspirations have not been fully or even partially realized, but I know the futility of dwelling on the past and the fruitlessness of daydreaming about the future. Please enable me to stay centered in the present moment. I desire to see your hand in sorrow as well as joy, for I believe that you can bring good even from the most painful situation.

Give me, in your mercy, the courage and strength to persevere in my desire to be a candle for you, no matter how insignificant my light may appear. I know that my heavenly Father sees all that is done in secret, no heartfelt prayer or honest deed has ever gone unnoticed. Each tiny candle adds to the illumination of the earth and brings our Father's kingdom closer to reality.

Jesus, I know that the evolution of my hidden self is a process involving time, patience, and openness to your presence. Thank you for all the ways your love is already enabling me to "grow strong so that Christ may live in my heart through faith." Then, "planted in love and built on love," I will with all the saints "have the strength to grasp the breadth and the length, the height and the depth, until, knowing the love of Christ, which is beyond all knowledge," I am "filled with the utter fullness of God" (Eph 3:17–19). AMEN.

CHAPTER EIGHT

SEASONED CITIZENS

I ALWAYS DREADED THE THOUGHT OF BECOMING A senior citizen. Then, one day I spotted a bumper sticker that gave me a different perspective. It said, "Age is only important to wine and cheese." Not long afterward I saw a plaque that announced, "Do not resist growing old. Many are denied the privilege." I knew my outlook needed an attitude adjustment.

I decided to adopt the term "seasoned citizen" for my new state in life. It seemed to better exemplify the outcome of my life's journey. I also refused to use the term "senior moment" when my brain wasn't able to recall certain information. Instead I referred to those moments as "intellectual interruptions." As one gentlemen remarked when he experienced a momentary lapse of memory, "My hard drive is operating okay but my data retrieval system just shut down!"

In his book, *I Don't Know What Old Is, But Old is Older Than Me,* eighty-two year old Sherwood Eliot Wirt, a retired Presbyterian minister, notes that Michelangelo was designing churches at eighty-eight, Albert Schweitzer was operating in his hospital in Africa at eighty-nine, Elizabeth Arden was still managing her cosmetics industry at eighty-five, and Mother Teresa was still caring for the poor until her death at eighty-seven.

According to the U.S. Census Bureau, there were 50,454 centenarians in the U.S. by 2000. That's a huge increase from the 1980 census when only 15,000 one-hundred-year-olds could be counted. In 1900, life expectancy was forty-nine years, today it's seventy-six. Those who study the science of gerontology observe the following common features among those who live to extreme old age:

a strong will and determined character
independence
sturdy personalities
positive outlook
sense of humor

Growing old can be a lot easier with strong religious beliefs according to several new studies. Researchers have discovered that elderly persons who are religiously active tend to be more optimistic and better able to cope with illness than people who are less religious. Another study found that even as people's physical ability declined, they still relied on their belief in God to combat loneliness and provide them with psychological support.

My friend, Amy, is an eighty-plus seasoned citizen living in Sun City, Arizona. She was diagnosed with polio when her fourth child was born and has been in wheel chair for more than forty years. Yet, she is a woman of deep faith who exudes joy and enthusiasm for life. On a recent visit, I asked the secret of her optimistic spiritual outlook. She smiled and said, "I don't believe God will allow me to make a liar out of him. He told us to 'ask and you will receive.' So each morning I spend time thanking God for my ability to see and hear and talk. I express my appreciation for all the healthy parts of my body. I don't spend a lot of time reminding the Lord of my disabilities because he's very much aware of those. I believe the Father responds to my 'attitude of gratitude' and this type of prayer gives me a positive attitude for the entire day."

Many years ago I found a prayer attributed to an anonymous seventeenth-century nun. It seemed quaint and charming at the time, but now I'm aware of the truth it expresses.

> Lord, Thou knowest better than I know myself that I am growing older and will someday—be old. Keep me from the fatal habit of thinking I must say something on every subject and on every occasion. Release me from craving to straighten out everybody's affairs. Make me thoughtful but not moody; helpful but not bossy. With my vast store of wisdom it seems a pity not to use it all, but Thou Lord knowest that I want a few friends at the end.

> Keep my mind free from the recital of endless details; give me wings to get to the point. Seal my lips on my aches and pains. They are increasing and love of rehearsing them is becoming sweeter as the years go by. I dare not ask for grace enough to enjoy the tales of others pains, but help me to endure them with patience. I dare not ask for an improved memory, but for a growing humility and a lessening cocksureness when my memory seems to clash with the memories of others. Teach me the glorious lesson that occasionally I may be mistaken.

> Keep me reasonably sweet; I do not want to be a Saint—some of them are so hard to live with—but a sour old person is one of the crowning works of the devil. Give me the ability to see good things in

unexpected places and talents in unexpected
people. And, give me, O Lord, the grace to tell
them so. Amen

St. Irenaeus in the second century said, "The glory of
God is man fully alive." The challenge faced by the elderly
in our society is to live life to the fullest, with our whole
being, until it's time to return home. It's well documented
that individuals stop growing when they stop learning. The
story is told that Franklin Delano Roosevelt, after his
inauguration in 1933, paid a courtesy call to the retired
jurist, Oliver Wendall Holmes, who was then more than
ninety. He found him reading Plato. When the President
asked him why he was reading the great philosopher, Mr.
Holmes replied, "To improve my mind, Mr. President."

I recall visiting the mother of a friend who, at the age of
eighty-three was a resident in a retirement home in
Cincinnati. She was bedridden, due to a hip injury, but was
busy reading the *Wall Street Journal* when I walked into her
room. For the next two hours we had a fascinating
discussion about current events and her view of the
solutions to the world's problems.

There is an Irish toast that says, "May you live all the
days of your life." It means cultivating all our God-given
resources for growth, becoming sensitive to the beauty
around us and the wonder of being a part of it. As one
preacher proclaimed, "Christians should have the abiding
joy of sharing, the extravagant rewards of loving, and the
bountiful harvest of believing."

The secret of living our life abundantly necessitates
bringing the experiences of our past into the light of God's
love. Some people arrive at this station in life full of
confidence. They accomplished their goals and are satisfied
with themselves. Others spend inordinate amounts of time

regretting the past and permitting feelings of hopelessness and despair to dominate their thinking. The incidence of suicide among the elderly in our country has been escalating in recent years.

Rabbi Morris Margolies in his book, *A Gathering of Angels,* shares an encounter he had in Nagasaki in 1952 with a survivor of the atomic bomb.

> I was on my way back to the States after having completed a tour of duty as a chaplain in Korea. I visited the Nagasaki museum, which depicts graphically some of what was wrought there on August 9, 1945. I found myself sobbing like an infant. A gentle touch on my arm turned my attention to a singular woman. She had one eye, one foot, one ear, and two crutches. She spoke to me in English, "Please, please do not weep for the dead and the torn. Weep instead for the living and the well. We have learned the ways of death. But we have not yet learned the way to life.

The sunset of our spiritual journey gives us an opportunity to take an inventory of our earthly life and ask Jesus to heal the areas that fall short of our original desires. Your children, if you had any, are grown and on their own. I always thought my responsibilities ended when they left the nest but I now know a parent's vocation is eternal. When God sends us offspring, he also anoints us with the spiritual power to intercede on their behalf.

In my daily prayer time I bring each of my children, their spouses, and the grandchildren into the presence of the Lord. I ask Jesus to make up whatever is lacking in my parenting skills. I pray that God will heal anything hurtful or painful between us and I thank him for bringing them into my life.

We cannot undervalue our role as teachers and guides for the younger generation. Several years ago my son, Chris, and his children were going through a difficult time. The family was breaking up because Chris' wife wanted a divorce. Five-year-old Sarah and seven-year-old Katie were very distraught. I bought each of them a rosary bracelet. As I placed the bracelets on their wrists, I reminded them of the Christmas story and how Mary cared for the infant Jesus.

"She is your Mother, too, and she'll never leave you," I explained. "You can tell her anything and she'll listen and comfort you." After their return home, I received a phone call from my son, Chris. He said, "Mom, the girls are talking to their bracelets all the time and it really seems to be helping. Thanks for knowing what to do."

It's estimated that there are currently ninety million grandparents in the United States. The role of influencing the grandchildren has never been more important. When my first grandson was born someone remarked, "God sends you children to teach you how to love and sends you grandchildren to love you back." I remember that observation whenever one of the little ones says, "I love you, Grandma."

Even if we are geographically separated we can still exert a presence in their lives through notes, e-mails, and phone calls. It can truly be one of the greatest joys of our twilight years.

Praying with seasoned citizens for inner healing usually opens up areas of heartache and grief. Most of us have had more than our share of sorrows which prevent us from enjoying our later years. Often these wounds are associated with the death of someone close to us. The pain associated with these losses can become debilitating if we fail to seek healing for the sorrow.

There is an ancient story which can put our grief into the proper perspective. It's told about a young woman named Kisa who experienced a series of tragedies. First her husband and another close family member died. All that remained for her was her only son. Then he was stricken with illness and died as well.

Wailing in grief, she carried the body of her child everywhere, asking for help, for medicine to bring him back to life, but no one would help her. Finally someone directed her to a rabbi who was teaching in a nearby forest grove.

She approached him, crying with grief, and said, "Great teacher, master, please bring my boy back to life." The rabbi replied, "I will do so, but first you must do something for me.

"You must go into the village and get me a handful of mustard seed (the most common spice). From this I will fashion a medicine for your child. There is one more thing, however," the Rabbi said. "The mustard seed must come from a home where no one has lost a child or a parent, a spouse or a friend."

Kisa ran into the village and into the first house begging for mustard seeds. "Please, please, may I have some?" And the people seeing her grief, responded immediately. But then she asked, "Has anyone in this home died? Has a mother or daughter or father or son?" They answered, "Yes, we had a death last year."

So Kisa ran to the next house. Again they willingly gave her the mustard seed and again she asked, "Has anyone here died?" This time it was the maiden aunt. And at the next house it was the young daughter who had died. And so it went, house after house in the village.

There was no household which had not known death.

Finally Kisa sat down in her sorrow and realized that what had happened to her and to her child happens to everyone, that all who are born will also die. She carried the body of her dead son back to the rabbi. There he was buried with proper rites.

She then asked the rabbi for teachings that would bring her wisdom and refuge in the realm of birth and death, and she herself took these teachings deeply to heart and became a wise woman.

I have discovered that there are many other ways for sadness to remain stuck in our hearts. In her book, *Necessary Losses*, Judith Viorst wrote:

> When we think of loss, we think of the loss through death of people we love. But loss is a far more encompassing theme in our life. For we lose not only through death but also by leaving and being left, by changing and letting go and moving on. And our losses include not only our separations and departures from those we love but our conscious and unconscious losses of romantic dreams, impossible expectations, illusions of freedom and power, illusions of safety and the loss of our own younger self—the self that thought it always would be unwrinkled and invulnerable and immortal.
>
> Passionate investment leaves us vulnerable to loss. And sometimes, no matter how clever we are, we must lose.
>
> Central to understanding our lives is understanding how we deal with loss.

Not long ago I visited a woman who was ninety-two years young. She shared her life story with me and I asked if she had any regrets. "Yes," she answered. "I always wanted to be a dancer, I love the ballet, but my mother said I was too clumsy and refused to allow me to take lessons." I prayed with her, asking Jesus to set her free from the feeling of loss. She began to weep as she imaged Jesus whirling her around a dance floor. The heaviness of spirit lifted and she felt peace. It wasn't many days later when she quietly departed this earth and, I'm convinced, she's dancing her way through heaven.

We can't go back in time to make a new start but we can start now to make a new end. The Reverend Martin Luther King, Jr., sums up the reason for our need to be healed when he said, "One day we will learn that the heart can never be totally right if the head is totally wrong. Only through bringing together and head and the heart, intelligence and goodness, shall man rise to a fulfillment of his true nature."

If we have desires this world fails to satisfy, it's helpful to remember that we weren't made for this world. The psalmist tells us, "The Lord is near to the brokenhearted, and saves the crushed in spirit" (Ps 34:18). When we place our sorrows into the hands of Jesus, they cease to bind us in depression.

The heartaches and sorrows of life may also bring feelings of anger against those who wounded us. There isn't anything that keeps us from experiencing the "peace that passes understanding" more than an unwillingness to forgive. Archbishop Desmond Tutu has lived most of his over seventy years with the barbarities of apartheid in South Africa. The torture, killings, degradation, and separation of families was a daily occurrence. He says, "It's not enough to say let bygones be bygones. We had to work and look the beast firmly in the eyes. Ultimately you discover that without forgiveness, there is no future. To forgive is the only way to permanently change the world."

Researchers say there is a physiological reason for forgiveness—health. At Hope College in Michigan, researchers measure heart rates, sweat rates, and other responses of subjects asked to remember past slights. They discovered that blood pressure increases, heart rate increases, and muscle tensions are also higher. This suggests their stress responses are greater during their unforgiving than forgiving conditions.

Those of us who want to live our lives to the fullest in our twilight years would do well to take a periodic spiritual inventory to see if we are holding on to unforgiveness toward others, ourselves, or even toward God.

One woman told me the story of her experience with this important spiritual tool. "When my husband got sick, he decided to take time to forgive everyone in his life, from his parents onward."

He made a list and name by name brought them to the foot of the cross where he prayed, "Jesus, from the cross you said, 'Father, forgive them for they do not know what they do.' Many who hurt me didn't even know how their behavior affected me. Give me the gift of forgiveness toward them." Thus he left this planet with a "clean heart."

After his death, his wife began using the same technique to forgive herself for not being there when he died, to forgive his doctors for letting him die, to forgive God for letting him die, to forgive him for dying, and on and on and on. She says, "Often, I have to go through this process several times before I can actually let go of my anger. This is especially true for his doctors. I use this technique for big things and for little things. When I use it with the little things, they don't get big.

It may seem strange to consider the need to forgive the all-loving God, yet it is possible to be angry at the Almighty for unanswered prayers, unfulfilled hopes, and unhappiness with our lot in life. The willingness to forgive brings blessings of renewed hope into our lives.

Some of us are afraid of growing old. Fear is a natural response whenever we encounter the unknown. The poet, Robert Browning, in his poem "Rabbi Ben Ezra" wrote,

Grow old along with me!
The best is yet to be.
The last of life, for which the first was made.
Our times are in His hand
Who saith, "A whole I planned,
Youth shows but half; trust God; see all nor be afraid.

My dear friend, Harriet, was my spiritual mother and a trusted advisor for most of my adult life. She introduced me to inner healing prayer and walked me through many of my life experiences to bring healing to my wounded heart. When she died a few years ago I was asked to speak at her funeral service. I shared some of my memories of her remarkable life and read the following:

A PARABLE OF IMMORTALITY
BY HENRY VAN DYKE

I am standing upon the seashore. A ship at my side spreads her white sails to the morning breeze and starts for the blue ocean. She is an object of beauty and strength, and I stand and watch until at last she hangs like a speck of white cloud just where the sun and sky come down to mingle with each other. Then someone at my side says, "There she goes!"

Gone where? Gone from my sight—that is all. She is just as large in mast and hull and spar as she was when she left my side and just as able to bear her load of living freight to the places of destination.

Her diminished size is in me, not in her. And just at the moment when someone at my side says, "There she goes!" there are other eyes watching

her coming and other voices ready to take up the
glad shout, "Here she comes!"

And so it will be for all of us. May the time remaining
to us on this earth be as richly fulfilling as possible.

DEAREST FATHER, I've arrived at the last portion of my earthly life. I'm carrying a lot of baggage that needs to be released. I remember your invitation to "come to me, all you who labor and are overburdened, and I will give you rest." So I bring to you those parts of me crying out for your touch. I give to you my feelings of disappointment regarding my unfulfilled hopes and dreams. Please forgive me for those moments when I selfishly wanted my own way and refused to love others as you bid me to do. Give me the grace to forgive those who have wounded me with their words and actions. Help me to deal with the inadequacies of my aging mind and body. Give me the grace to be blessing to those around me and not resent their attempts to assist me. Let me cherish my life experiences and share them in meaningful ways since I am a "living ancestor" to the younger generation. Thank you for the gift of life given to me so long ago. May my earthly journey leave a legacy of love to all who know me. AMEN.

PRAYER

EPILOGUE

INNER HEALING IS A LIFETIME PROCESS REQUIRING our willingness to invite Jesus Christ to heal our hidden selves. The following story illustrates the importance of our participation in the process.

Two seeds lay side by side in the fertile spring soil.

The first said, "I want to grow! I want to send my roots into the soil beneath me, and thrust my sprouts through the earth's crust above me. I want to unfurl my tender buds like banners to announce the arrival of spring. I want to feel the warmth of the sun on my face and the blessing of the morning dew on my petals!"

And so she grew.

The second seed said, "I am afraid. If I send my roots into the ground below, I don't know what I will encounter in the dark. If I push my way through the hard soil above me I may damage my delicate sprouts. What if I let my buds open and a snail tries to eat them? And if I were to open my blossoms, a small child may pull me from the ground. No, it is much better for me to wait until it is safe."

And so she waited.

A yard hen scratching around in the early spring ground for food found the waiting seed and promptly ate it.

The moral of the story? Those of us who refuse to risk and grow get swallowed up by life.

We cannot begin inner transformation unless we're open to change. Yet most of us are resistant to any form of alteration in our lives. We prefer to stay as we are rather than risk what might be. Indeed, the only one who usually welcomes change is a wet baby.

Being patient with the evolution of our true self is also an important component of inner healing. At our home in Florida we have a citrus tree we have lovingly tended for several years. This year the grapefruit tree brought out its blossoms too early. The fruit grew too quickly and when Florida experienced record-breaking heat this summer, nearly all the grapefruit burst and fell from the tree. Rather than ripening slowly, the fruit literally exploded from within.

It is worth noting that the beloved Twenty-Third Psalm says: *"Yea, though I walk through the valley of the shadow of death."* We can't fly over the valley, detour around it, nor run through it. We have to walk. One step at a time. One lonely night at a time.

The prophet Micah points out the pathway of our journey toward wholeness. "What does the Lord require of you? Only to do justice, to love mercy, and to walk humbly with your God" (Mi 6:8). Learning to live in harmony with ourselves and others is a goal to be attained throughout our earthly lives.

On display at the French Academy of Science in Paris is a shoemaker's awl. It's an ordinary pointed tool used to make holes in leather but behind the little awl are both tragedy and victory. It fell one day from the shoemaker's workbench and put out the eye of his little nine-year-old son. Within weeks the child was blind in both eyes and had to attend a special school for the sightless. At that time the blind learned to read by using large carved wooden blocks that were awkward to handle. When the shoemaker's son grew up, he devised a new reading system of punched dots on paper. And to do it, Louis Braille used the same awl that had blinded him.

As Jesus heals the wounds of our past they can become a source of compassion and understanding for the world around us. We don't forget what has happened but we now view our experiences through the wounds of our Savior. They can no longer hold us captive. We have been freed by the blood of the Lamb.

In Jesus the proclamation of the prophet Isaiah was fulfilled, "Yahweh has anointed me to bring good news to the poor, to bind up hearts that are broken, to proclaim liberty to captives, and to comfort all those who mourn" (Is 61:1–3).

We will truly find our hidden self as we open our hearts and minds to the gentle touch of Jesus Christ.

SOURCES

These sources are listed, by title, in the order that they appear in the text.

Whatever Became of Sin?, Karl Menninger, Bantam Books, New York, NY, 1988.

The Power in Penance, Michael Scanlan, Ave Maria Press, Notre Dame, IN, 1972.

Birth Without Violence, Dr. Frederick Leboyer, Alfred A. Knopf, Publisher, New York, 1975.

The Birth Book, by William and Martha Sears, published by authors, 1994.

A Good Birth, a Safe Birth, Diane Korte and Roberta Scaer, Harvard Common Press, Boston, MA, 1992.

Maternal-Infant Bonding, Drs. Marshall Klaus and John Kennell, published by C.V. Mosby, St. Louis, MO, 1976.

Life in the Middle Ages, C.G. Coulton, ed Macmillian, New York, 1910.

Touching: The Human Significance of the Skin, Ashley Montague, Harper and Row, New York, NY, 1971.

A report by Dr. T. Berry Brazelton, *Redbook* magazine, April, 1981.

The Conspiracy Against Childhood, Eda LaShan, MacMillan Publishing Co., New York, NY, 1971.

Association of Christian Therapists, 6728 Old McLean Village Drive, McLean, VA 22101. The Web site is: www.actheals.org

Betrayal of Innocence, Susan Ford and Craig Bush, Penguin Books, New York, NY, 1988.

Good Grief, Granger Westberg, Fortress Press, Minneapolis, MN, 1962.

A Cry Unheard: New Insights Into the Medical Consequences of Loneliness, James Lynch, Bancroft Press, Baltimore, MD, 2000.

Healing the Wounds of Divorce, Barbara Shlemon Ryan, Ave Maria Press, Notre Dame, IN, 1992.

I Don't Know What Old Is, But Old Is Older Than Me, Sherwood Eliot Wirt, Thomas Nelson Publisher, Nashville, TN, 1992.

A Gathering of Angels, Morris Margolies, Ballantine Books, New York, NY, 1994.

Necessary Losses, Judith Viorst, Ballantine Books, New York, NY, 1986.

The Works of Henry Van Dyke, Charles Scribner's Sons, New York, 1921.

 BARBARA SHLEMON RYAN
is President of Beloved
Ministry and has been
actively involved in the
healing ministry since 1965.
She travels nationally and
internationally as a retreat
director, conference speaker
and workshop leader.

Ryan is one of the
founding members of the
Association of Christian
Therapists, an international
organization of professionals
in the physical, mental and
spiritual health care fields who seek to integrate faith
experience with their medical expertise. She is also the
author of several books including *Healing the Wounds of
Divorce* (Ave Maria Press), *Healing Prayer: Spiritual
Pathways to Health and Wellness* (Charis Books), *Living
Each Day by the Power of Faith: Thirty Meditations to
Deepen Your Trust in God* (Resurrection Press Ltd).

Ryan is the mother of five grown children and is also a
grandmother.

LaVergne, TN USA
31 March 2011
222182LV00002B/142/P